TIMED READINGS PLUS

25 Two-Part Lessons
with Questions for
Building Reading Speed and Comprehension

BOOK THREE

Edward Spargo

JAMESTOWN PUBLISHERS

a division of NTC/CONTEMPORARY PUBLISHING GROUP
Lincolnwood, Illinois USA

Timed Readings Plus, Book Three, Level F
Selection text adapted from Compton's Encyclopedia.
Used with permission of Compton's Learning Company.

ISBN: 0-89061-905-0

Published by Jamestown Publishers,
a division of NTC/Contemporary Publishing Group, Inc.,
4255 West Touhy Avenue,
Lincolnwood, Illinois, 60712 U.S.A.

01 02 03 04 ML 12 11 10 9 8 7 6 5 4

CONTENTS

To the Instructor

Overview

Timed Readings Plus is designed to develop both reading speed and comprehension. A timed selection in each lesson focuses on improving reading rate. A nontimed selection—the "plus" selection—follows the timed selection. The nontimed selection concentrates on building mastery in critical areas of comprehension.

The 10 books in the series span reading levels 4–13, with one book at each level. Readability of the selections was assessed by using the Fry Readability Scale. Each book contains 25 lessons; each lesson is divided into Parts A and B.

Part A includes the timed selection followed by 10 multiple-choice questions: 5 fact questions and 5 thought questions. The timed selection is 400 words long and contains subject matter that is factual, nonfiction, and textbook-like. Because everyone—regardless of level—reads a 400-word passage, the steps for the timed selection can be concurrent for everyone.

Part B includes the nontimed selection, which is more narrative than the timed selection. The length of the selection varies depending on the subject matter, which relates to the content of the timed selection. The nontimed selection is followed by five comprehension questions that address the following major comprehension skills: recognizing words in context, distinguishing fact from opinion, keeping events in order, making correct inferences, and understanding main ideas.

Getting Started

Begin by assigning students to a level. A student should start with a book that is one level below his or her current reading level. If a student's reading level is not known, a suitable starting point would be one or two levels below the student's present grade in school.

Teaching a Lesson: Part A

Work in each lesson begins with the timed selection in Part A. If you wish to have all the students in the class read a selection at the same time, you can coordinate the timing using the following method. Give students the signal to preview. Allow 15 seconds for this. Have students begin reading the selection at the same time. After one minute has passed, write on the chalkboard the time that has elapsed. Update the time at 10-second intervals (1:00, 1:10, 1:20, etc.). Tell students to copy down the last time shown on the chalkboard when they finish reading. They should then record this reading time in the space designated after the selection.

If students keep track of their own reading times, have them write the times at which they start and finish reading on a separate piece of paper and then figure and record their reading time as above.

Students should now answer the ten questions that follow the Part A selection. Responses are recorded by putting an X in the box next to the student's choice of answer. Correct responses to eight or more questions indicates satisfactory comprehension and recall.

Teaching a Lesson: Part B

When students have finished Part A, they can move on to read the Part B selection. Although brief, these selections deliver all the content needed to attack the range of comprehension questions that follow.

Students next answer the comprehension questions that follow the Part B selection. Directions for answering the questions are provided with each question. Correct responses require deliberation and discrimination.

Correcting and Scoring Answers

Using the Answer Key at the back of the book, students self-score their responses to the questions in Parts A and B. Incorrect answers should be circled and the correct answers should be marked. The number of correct answers for Part A and for Part B and the total correct answers should be tallied on the final page of the lesson.

Using the Graphs

Reading times are plotted on the Reading Rate graph at the back of the book. The legend on the graph automatically converts reading times to words-per-minute rates. Comprehension totals are plotted on the Comprehension Scores graph. Plotting automatically converts the raw scores to a comprehension percentage based on four points per correct answer.

Diagnosis and Evaluation

The Comprehension Skills Profile graph at the back of the book tracks student responses to the Part B comprehension questions. For each incorrect response, students should mark an X in the corresponding box on the graph. A column of Xs rising above other columns indicates a specific comprehension weakness. Using the profile, you can assess trends in student performance and suggest remedial work if necessary.

A student who has reached a peak in reading speed (with satisfactory comprehension) is ready to advance to the next book in the series. Before moving on to the next book, students should be encouraged to maintain their speed and comprehension on a number of lessons in order to consolidate their achievement.

How to Use This Book

Getting Started

Study Part A: Reading Faster and Better. Read and learn the steps to follow and the techniques to use to help you read more quickly and more efficiently.

Study Part B: Mastering Reading Comprehension. Learn what the five categories of comprehension are all about. Knowing what kind of comprehension response is expected from you and how to achieve that response will help you better comprehend all you read.

Working a Lesson

Find the Starting Lesson. Locate the timed selection in Part A of the lesson that you are going to read. Wait for your instructor's signal to preview the selection. Your instructor will allow you 15 seconds for previewing.

Read the Part A Selection. When your instructor gives you the signal, begin reading. Read at a faster-than-normal speed. Read carefully so that you will be able to answer questions about what you have read.

Record Your Reading Time. When you finish reading, look at the blackboard and note your reading time. Write this time at the bottom of the page on the line labeled Reading Time.

Answer the Part A Questions. Answer the 10 questions that follow the selection. There are 5 fact questions and 5 thought questions. Choose the best answer to each question and put an X in that box.

Read the Part B Selection. This passage is less textbook-like and more story-like than the timed selection. Read well enough so that you can answer the questions that follow.

Answer the Part B Questions. These questions are different from traditional multiple-choice questions. In answering these questions, you must make three choices for each question. Instructions for answering each category of question are given. There are 15 responses for you to record.

Correct Your Answers. Use the Answer Key at the back of the book. For the Part A questions, circle any wrong answer and put an X in the box you should have marked. For the Part B questions, circle any wrong answer and write the correct letter or number next to it.

Scoring Your Work

Total Your Correct Answers. Count your correct answers for Part A and for Part B. Record those numbers on the appropriate lines at the end of the lesson. Then add the two scores to determine your total correct answers. Record that number on the appropriate line.

Plotting Your Progress

Plot Your Reading Time. Refer to the Reading Rate graph on page 116. On the vertical line that represents your lesson, put an X at the point where it intersects your reading time, shown along the left-hand side. The right-hand side of the graph will reveal your words-per-minute reading speed. Your instructor will review this graph from time to time to evaluate your progress.

Plot Your Comprehension Scores. Record your comprehension scores on the graph on page 117. On the vertical line that represents your lesson, put an X at the point where it intersects your total correct answers, shown along the left-hand side. The right-hand side of the graph will reveal your comprehension percentage. Your instructor will want to review this graph, too. Your achievement, as shown on both graphs, will determine your readiness to move on to higher and more challenging levels.

Plot Your Comprehension Skills. You will find the Comprehension Skills Profile on page 118. It is used to record your wrong answers only for the Part B questions. The five categories of questions are listed along the bottom. There are five columns of boxes, one column for each question. For every wrong answer, put an X in a box for that question. Your instructor will use this graph to detect any comprehension problems you may be experiencing.

Part A: Reading Faster and Better

Step 1: Preview

When you read, do you start in with the first word, or do you look over the whole selection for a moment? Good readers preview the selection first. This helps make them good—and fast—readers. Here are the steps to follow when previewing the timed selection in Part A of each unit.

1. Read the Title. Titles are designed not only to announce the subject, but also to make the reader think. What can you learn from the title? What thoughts does it bring to mind? What do you already know about this subject?

2. Read the First Sentence. Read the first two sentences if they are short. The opening sentence is the writer's opportunity to greet the reader. Some writers announce what they hope to tell you in the selection. Some writers tell you why they are writing. Other writers just try to get your attention.

3. Read the Last Sentence. Read the final two sentences if they are short. The closing sentence is the writer's last chance to talk to you. Some writers repeat the main idea once more. Some writers draw a conclusion—this is what they have been leading up to. Other writers summarize their thoughts; they tie all the facts together.

4. Scan the Selection. Glance through the selection quickly to see what else you can pick up. Look for anything that can help you read the selection. Are there names, dates, or numbers? If so, you may have to read more slowly. Is the selection informative—containing a lot of facts, or is it conversational—an informal discussion with the reader?

Step 2: Read for Meaning

When you read, do you just see words? Are you so occupied reading words that you sometimes fail to get the meaning? Good readers see beyond the words—they seek the meaning. This makes them faster readers.

1. Build Concentration. You cannot read with understanding if you are not concentrating. When you discover that your thoughts are straying, correct the situation right away. Avoid distractions and distracting situations. Keep the preview information in mind. This will help focus your attention on the selection.

2. Read in Thought Groups. A reader should strive to see words in meaningful combinations. If you see only a word at a time (called word-by-word reading), your comprehension suffers along with your speed.

3. Question the Writer. To sustain the pace you have set for yourself, and to maintain a high level of concentration and comprehension, question the writer as you read. Ask yourself such questions as, "What does this mean? How can I use this information?"

Step 3: Grasp Paragraph Sense

The paragraph is the basic unit of meaning. If you can discover quickly and understand the main point of each paragraph, you can comprehend the writer's message. Good readers know how to find the main ideas quickly. This helps make them faster readers.

1. Find the Topic Sentence. The topic sentence, which contains the main idea, is often the first sentence of a paragraph. It is followed by sentences that support, develop, or explain the main idea. Sometimes a topic sentence comes at the end of a paragraph. When it does, the supporting details come first, building the base for the topic sentence. Some paragraphs do not have a topic sentence; all of the sentences combine to create a meaningful idea.

2. Understand Paragraph Structure. Every well-written paragraph has a purpose. The purpose may be to inform, define, explain, illustrate, and so on. The purpose should always relate to the main idea and expand on it. As you read each paragraph, see how the body of the paragraph is used to tell you more about the main idea.

Step 4: Organize Facts

When you read, do you tend to see a lot of facts without any apparent connection or relationship? Understanding how the facts all fit together to deliver the writer's message is, after all, the reason for reading. Good readers organize facts as they read. This helps them read rapidly and well.

1. Discover the Writer's Plan. Every writer has a plan or outline to follow. If you can discover the writer's method of organization, you have a key to understanding the message. Sometimes the writer gives you obvious signals. The statement, "There are three reasons . . .," should prompt you to look for a listing of the three items. Other less obvious signal words such as *moreover, otherwise,* and *consequently* tell you the direction the writer is taking in delivering a message.

2. Relate as You Read. As you read the selection, keep the information learned during the preview in mind. See how the writer is attempting to piece together a meaningful message. As you discover the relationship among the ideas, the message comes through quickly and clearly.

Part B: Mastering Reading Comprehension

Recognizing Words in Context

Always check to see if the words around a new word—its context—can give you some clue to its meaning. A word generally appears in a context related to its meaning. If the words *soil* and *seeds* appear in an article about gardens, for example, you can assume they are related to the topic of gardens.

Suppose you are unsure of the meaning of the word *expired* in the following paragraph:

> Vera wanted to take a book out, but her library card had expired.
> She had to borrow mine because she didn't have time to renew hers.

You could begin to figure out the meaning of *expired* by asking yourself, "What could have happened to Vera's library card that would make her have to borrow someone else's card?" You might realize that if she had to renew her card, it must have come to an end or run out. This would lead you to conclude that the word *expired* must mean to come to an end or run out. You would be right. The context suggested the meaning to you.

Context can also affect the meaning of a word you know. The word *key*, for instance, has many meanings. There are musical keys, door keys, and keys to solving a mystery. The context in which *key* occurs will tell you which meaning is right.

Sometimes a hard word will be explained by the words that immediately follow it. The word *grave* in the following sentence might give you trouble:

> He looked grave; there wasn't a trace of a smile on his lips.

You can figure out that the second part of the sentence explains the word *grave:* "wasn't a trace of a smile" indicates a serious look, so *grave* must mean serious.

The subject of a sentence and your knowledge about that subject might also help you determine the meaning of an unknown word. Try to decide the meaning of the word *revive* in the following sentence:

> Sunshine and water will revive those drooping plants.

The sentence is about giving plants light and water. You may know that plants need light and water to be healthy. If you know that drooping plants are not healthy, you can figure out that *revive* means to bring back to health.

Distinguishing Fact from Opinion

Every day you are called upon to sort out fact and opinion. When a friend says she saw Mel Gibson's greatest movie last night, she is giving you her opinion. When she says she saw Mel Gibson's latest movie, she may be stating a fact. The fact can be proved—you can check to confirm or verify that the movie is indeed Mel Gibson's most recent film. The opinion can be disputed—ask around and others may not agree about the film's unqualified greatness. Because much of what you read and hear contains both facts and opinions, you need to be able to tell them apart. You need the skill of distinguishing fact from opinion.

Facts are statements that can be proved true. The proof must be objective and verifiable. You must be able to check for yourself to confirm a fact.

Look at the following facts. Notice that they can be checked for accuracy and confirmed. Suggested sources for verification appear in parentheses.

- In 1998 Bill Clinton was president of the United States. (Consult newspapers, news broadcasts, election results, etc.)

- Earth revolves around the sun. (Look it up in encyclopedias or astrological journals; ask knowledgeable people.)

- Dogs walk on four legs. (See for yourself.)

Opinions are statements that cannot be proved true. There is no objective evidence you can consult to check the truthfulness of an opinion. Unlike facts, opinions express personal beliefs or judgments. Opinions reveal how someone feels about a subject, not the facts about that subject. You might agree or disagree with someone's opinion, but you cannot prove it right or wrong.

Look at the following opinions. Reasons for classification as opinions appear in parentheses.

- Bill Clinton was born to be a president. (You cannot prove this by referring to birth records. There is no evidence to support this belief.)

- Intelligent life exists on other planets in our solar system. (There is no proof of this. It may be proved true some day, but for now it is just an educated guess—not a fact.)

- Dog is man's best friend. (This is not a fact; your best friend might not be a dog.)

As you read, be aware that facts and opinions are frequently mixed together. The following passage contains both facts and opinions:

> The new 2000 Cruising Yacht offers lots of real-life interior room. It features a luxurious aft cabin, not some dim "cave." The galley

comes equipped with a full-size refrigerator and freezer. And this spacious galley has room to spare. The heads (there are two) have separate showers. The fit and finish are beyond equal and the performance is responsive and outstanding.

Did you detect that the third and fifth sentences state facts and that the rest of the sentences express opinions? Both facts and opinions are useful to you as a reader. But to evaluate what you read and to read intelligently, you need to know the difference between them.

Keeping Events in Order

Writers organize details in a pattern. They present information in a certain order. Recognizing how writers organize—and understanding that organization—can help you improve your comprehension.

When details are arranged in the precise order in which they occurred, a writer is using a chronological (or time) pattern. A writer may, however, change this order. The story may "flash back" to past events that affected the present. The story may "flash forward" to show the results of present events. The writer may move back and forth between past, present, and future to help you see the importance of events.

Making Correct Inferences

Much of what you read suggests more than it says. Writers do not always state outright what they want you to know. Frequently, they omit information that underlies the statements they make. They may assume that you already know it. They may want you to make the effort to figure out the implied information. To get the most out of what you read, you must come to an understanding about unstated information. You can do this through inference. From what is stated, you make inferences about what is not.

You make many inferences every day. Imagine, for example, that you are visiting a friend's house for the first time. You see a bag of dog food. You infer (make an inference) that the family has a dog. On another day you overhear a conversation. You catch the names of two actors and the words *scene, dialogue,* and *directing.* You infer that the people are discussing a movie or play.

In these situations and others like them, you infer unstated information from what you observe or read. Readers who cannot make inferences cannot see beyond the obvious. For the careful reader, facts are just the beginning. Facts stimulate your mind to think beyond them—to make an inference about what is meant but not stated.

The following passage is about Charles Dickens. As you read it, see how many inferences you can make.

Charles Dickens visited the United States in 1867. Wherever he went, the reception was the same. The night before, crowds arrived and lined up before the door. By morning the streets were campgrounds, with men, women, and children sitting or sleeping on blankets. Hustlers got ten times the price of a ticket. Once inside, audiences were surprised to hear their favorite Dickens characters speak with an English accent. After 76 readings Dickens boarded a ship for England. When his fellow passengers asked him to read, he said he'd rather be put in irons!

Did you notice that many inferences may be drawn from the passage? Dickens attracted huge crowds. From that fact you can infer that he was popular. His English accent surprised audiences. You can infer that many people didn't know he was English. Hustlers got high prices for tickets. This suggests that "scalping" tickets is not new. Dickens refused to read on the ship. You can infer that he was exhausted and tired of reading aloud to audiences. Those are some obvious inferences that can be made from the passage. More subtle ones can also be made; however, if you see the obvious ones, you understand how inferences are made.

Be careful about the inferences you make. One set of facts may suggest several inferences. Not all of them will be correct; some will be faulty inferences. The correct inference is supported by enough evidence to make it more likely than other inferences.

Understanding Main Ideas

The main idea tells who or what is the subject of the paragraph or passage. The main idea is the most important idea, the idea that provides purpose and direction. The rest of the paragraph or passage explains, develops, or supports the main idea. Without a main idea, there would be only a collection of unconnected thoughts. It would be like a handle and a bowl without the "idea cup," or bread and meat without the "idea sandwich."

In the following passage, the main idea is printed in italics. As you read, observe how the other sentences develop or explain the main idea.

> *Typhoon Chris hit with full fury today on the central coast of Japan.* Heavy rain from the storm flooded the area. High waves carried many homes into the sea. People now fear that the heavy rains will cause mudslides in the central part of the country. The number of people killed by the storm may climb past the 200 mark by Saturday.

In this paragraph, the main idea statement appears first. It is followed by sentences that explain, support, or give details. Sometimes the main idea appears at the end of a paragraph. Writers often construct that type of paragraph when their purpose is to persuade or convince. Readers may be more open to a new idea if the reasons for it are presented first. As you read the following paragraph, think about the overall impact of the supporting ideas. Their purpose is to convince the reader that the main idea in the last sentence should be accepted.

> Last week there was a head-on collision at Huntington and Canton streets. Just a month ago a pedestrian was struck there. Fortunately, she was only slightly injured. In the past year there have been more accidents there than at any other corner in the city. In fact, nearly 10 percent of all city accidents occur there. This intersection is dangerous, and a traffic signal should be installed there before a life is lost.

The details in the paragraph progress from least important to most important. They achieve their full effect in the main idea statement at the end.

In many cases, the main idea is not expressed in a single sentence. The reader is called upon to interpret all of the ideas expressed and decide upon a main idea. Read the following paragraph:

> The American author Jack London was once a pupil at the Cole Grammar School in Oakland, California. Each morning the class sang a song. When the teacher noticed that Jack wouldn't sing, she sent him to the principal. He returned to class with a note. It said that he could be excused from singing if he would write an essay every morning.

In this paragraph, the reader has to interpret the individual ideas and decide on a main idea. This main idea seems reasonable: Jack London's career as a writer began with a "punishment" in grammar school.

Understanding the concept of the main idea and knowing how to find it is important. Transferring that understanding to your reading and study is also important.

Preserved in Rock

Fossils tell the story of animals that lived long, long ago. If it were not for fossils, no one would know about the dinosaurs that once walked the earth. Without fossils, no one know about the great woolly mammoths or other now extinct animals. People's knowledge of ancient plants comes from fossils, too. Fossils are traces of once living things found in rocks.

Many different kinds of fossils have been found around the earth. Some fossils are whole animals. The animals were buried in such a way that air could not reach their bodies. This kept their bodies from decaying. For example, many insects of long ago were trapped in the resin of ancient pine trees. After the insects were trapped, the resin hardened, was buried underground, and became amber. The insects remained unchanged. The resin preserved them. Today, they still look very much as they did when they were trapped millions of years ago. Many museums have collections that include insects encased in amber.

A few woolly mammoths have been found frozen in the far north. They were frozen in great blocks of ice left from the last Ice Age. Of course, these mammoths decayed very rapidly when they were broken out of their icy tombs.

Fossil footprints are imprints made by dinosaurs or other animals when they walked across a layer of soft mud. Usually, footprints were washed away or spoiled by other footprints. But at times, conditions were such that the footprints were not destroyed. When the mud hardened into solid rock, the footprints remained.

Some fossils are simply the hard parts of plants or animals that have been preserved. A fossil, for instance, may be a shell or a bone that has remained unchanged. From the tar pits of California have come great quantities of bones. The tar has preserved the bones.

Some ancient animals bones have petrified. When an animal dies, the soft parts of its body decay rather rapidly. The bones remain for a longer time. Sometimes the bones are buried in sandy mud or in mud with a lime content. Water in the mud gradually dissolves the bone material and deposits some rock material in its place. Little by little, then, a true bone becomes a bone of stone. *Petrified* means "turned to stone." A petrified bone is not actually one that is turned to stone. The bone is really rebuilt in stone.

Reading Time _____

Recalling Facts

1. Amber is formed when
   - ❏ a. resin is buried underground for a very long time.
   - ❏ b. ancient insects are buried under rocks.
   - ☑ c. pine trees decay.

2. A fossil is a trace of a once living thing that has been
   - ☑ a. preserved.
   - ❏ b. altered by time.
   - ❏ c. destroyed.

3. Fossils provide information about
   - ❏ a. the solar system.
   - ☑ b. ancient animals and plants.
   - ❏ c. early inventions.

4. In the far north, woolly mammoths have been found encased in
   - ❏ a. tar.
   - ❏ b. amber.
   - ☑ c. ice.

5. An object that is petrified has been rebuilt in
   - ❏ a. mud.
   - ☑ b. stone.
   - ❏ c. tar.

Understanding Ideas

6. You can conclude from the article that fossils can be
   - ❏ a. found mainly in areas with cold climates.
   - ☑ b. formed in many different ways.
   - ❏ c. made only of stone.

7. You can conclude that fossils provide valuable information about
   - ❏ a. how people lived in the past.
   - ❏ b. the different kinds of rocks.
   - ☑ c. the kinds of plants and animals that lived long ago.

8. The biggest danger to fossils is most likely
   - ❏ a. time.
   - ☑ b. air.
   - ❏ c. modern technology.

9. By studying fossils, scientists are unlikely to learn much about
   - ❏ a. the age of an animal.
   - ❏ b. an animal's size.
   - ☑ c. an animal's internal organs.

10. You can conclude that scientists
    - ❏ a. have found all of the earth's fossils.
    - ☑ b. will continue to find and to learn from fossils.
    - ❏ c. learn little from fossil discoveries.

Caren Chase has an exciting job. She works for a museum as a fossil preparer. She travels to places where fossils are found. There, she makes sure they are dug up and shipped carefully.

Chase's latest trip was to Mongolia's Gobi Desert. Some of the world's best-preserved dinosaurs lie under the Gobi's sand. Getting a dinosaur skeleton safely out of its surrounding rock requires many hands, and Chase is there to see that the job is done right.

Chase collects specimens herself. On the Gobi trip, she found a five-inch (12.7-cm) lizard fossil. She brushed away the sand. She cut into the rock around the lizard, not too close to the actual specimen. When the block of soft rock with the lizard inside was almost free, she covered it with gauze and a layer of plaster of paris. Then she pulled the block free and flipped it over. She coated the underside with plaster of paris, too. The plaster kept the fossil safe on its journey to the museum.

Back at the museum, Chase carefully chipped away the plaster and the rock to expose the delicate fossil skeleton. Preserved and prepared, it would become part of the museum's display of prehistoric life.

1. Recognizing Words in Context

Find the word *close* in the passage. One definition below is a *synonym* for that word; it means the same or almost the same thing. One definition is an *antonym;* it has the opposite or nearly opposite meaning. The other has a completely different meaning. Label the definitions S for *synonym*, A for *antonym*, and D for *different.*

D a. stuffy
A b. far
S c. near

2. Distinguishing Fact from Opinion

Two of the statements below present *facts,* which can be proved correct. The other statement is an *opinion,* which expresses someone's thoughts or beliefs. Label the statements F for *fact* and O for *opinion.*

O a. Caren Chase's job is exciting.
F b. Caren Chase works as a fossil preparer.
F c. Caren Chase traveled to the Gobi Desert.

3. Keeping Events in Order

Label the statements below 1, 2, and 3 to show the order in which the events happened.

___3___ a. Caren covered the block with gauze and a layer of plaster of paris.

___2___ b. Caren brushed away the sand and cut into the rock around the fossil.

___1___ c. Caren found a lizard fossil.

4. Making Correct Inferences

Two of the statements below are correct *inferences,* or reasonable guesses. They are based on information in the passage. The other statement is an incorrect, or faulty, inference. Label the statements C for *correct* inference and F for *faulty* inference.

_____ a. Fossils can be damaged easily.

_____ b. Even small fossil specimens require special handling.

_____ c. No special training is necessary to dig for fossils.

5. Understanding Main Ideas

One of the statements below expresses the main idea of the passage. One statement is too general, or too broad. The other explains only part of the passage; it is too narrow. Label the statements M for *main idea,* B for *too broad,* and N for *too narrow.*

_____ a. Caren Chase's latest trip for her museum was to Mongolia's Gobi Desert.

_____ b. In the Gobi Desert on a fossil hunt, fossil preparer Caren Chase found a lizard fossil and prepared it for shipment to her museum.

_____ c. Some of the world's best-preserved dinosaur fossils lie under the Gobi Desert.

Correct Answers, Part A _____

Correct Answers, Part B _____

Total Correct Answers _____

The Need for Power

The speed with which a machine does its work depends upon the kind of power driving it. At first, people turned cranks, worked pedals, or pulled on ropes to operate machines. People pushed the bars of a windlass. A windlass is a kind of drum that winds up a rope as it turns. It is used to lift and pull heavy loads.

Early machines depended upon the power people provided. The machines slowed down as human muscles got tired. Later horses, cattle, and even dogs were used to power treadmills and windlasses. The animals had more endurance than humans. But they, too, were living creatures that grew tired. This is why some other kind of power was needed for machines to reach their full usefulness.

Then someone thought of harnessing the power of wind and water. Windmills and waterwheels became the chief sources of power until well into the nineteenth century. They were used to pump water, grind grain, press oil, and work the machinery used in factories. Water and wind power was a big improvement over people and animals. But these sources had their limitations, too. When the wind died, windmill arms slowed and stopped turning. During times of drought, there was not enough water to turn waterwheels. A better source of energy was needed to operate machines.

In the mid-1700s, a young Scot named James Watt thought of a different source of power. The idea came to him as he watched steam rising from a teakettle. Why couldn't steam power be used to run machines? As he grew older, Watts experimented with steam engines. Finally, he succeeded in inventing a practical steam engine that had many uses. It was used to pump water from the tunnels of coal mines. It was used to operate machines in factories. It turned the grindstones in flour mills. When the steam engine was mounted on wheels, it could pull cars along a track.

With the steam engine, factories had a better source of power. The steam engine was always ready to go. If more power was needed, bigger engines could be built to supply it.

Then, in the last half of the nineteenth century, an entirely new source of power—electricity—came into use. Now the time was really ripe for the machine age. With a dependable supply of steam and electricity, machines could be designed to do all sorts of things.

Reading Time 1 : 53

Recalling Facts

1. To do work, machines depend on
   - ❏ a. switches.
   - ❏ b. orders.
   - ☑ c. power.

2. A windlass is a machine that is used to
   - ❏ a. press oil.
   - ☑ b. lift loads.
   - ❏ c. produce steam.

3. The chief sources of power during much of the nineteenth century were
   - ❏ a. humans.
   - ❏ b. animals.
   - ❏ c. water and wind.

4. A waterwheel is not a good source of power when
   - ☑ a. there is a drought.
   - ❏ b. muscles tire.
   - ❏ c. the wind dies down.

5. James Watt invented the
   - ❏ a. waterwheel.
   - ☑ b. practical steam engine.
   - ❏ c. electricity.

Understanding Ideas

6. You can conclude from the article that early machines
   - ❏ a. were not very useful.
   - ☑ b. required great muscle power.
   - ❏ c. helped do work faster.

7. Natural sources of power, such as wind and water, are a problem because they
   - ☑ a. are undependable.
   - ❏ b. are expensive.
   - ❏ c. grow tired.

8. You can conclude that windmills worked best
   - ☑ a. in open areas.
   - ❏ b. inside large buildings.
   - ❏ c. near a water source.

9. Because of changes in power sources, machines have become
   - ☑ a. more useful.
   - ❏ b. less helpful.
   - ❏ c. unneeded.

10. An advantage of electricity and steam as power sources is
    - ❏ a. roughness.
    - ☑ b. economy.
    - ❏ c. reliability.

The Wind Ball That Worked

James Watt invented the first practical steam engine in 1769. However, this was not the world's first steam engine. In the first century A.D., Hero of Alexandria described one of his inventions. This Greco-Egyptian mathematician and engineer called it an aeolopile, or "wind ball." The "wind ball" was the very first steam engine.

Hero did not think his steam engine had a practical use. He saw it only as an interesting device. However, he is credited with a long list of other inventions. He designed surveying instruments and mechanical puppet theaters. He invented a fire engine and organs powered by water and wind. He even made doors that opened automatically!

It was Hero's steam engine that interested Dr. J. G. Landels, a professor at a British university. He wanted to find out if the "wind ball" would work. He hoped to learn whether it might have had a useful purpose. With the help of the school's engineering department, Landels built a model of the engine. It worked! But it was not practical. Landels estimated that the engine was only about one percent efficient. It needed huge amounts of fuel—firewood or charcoal—to heat water and produce steam. It would take a lot of work and time to collect the fuel needed for a large "wind ball." The amount of work the wind ball could do would not make up for the time and work needed to supply fuel.

1. **Recognizing Words in Context**

   Find the word *produce* in the passage. One definition below is a *synonym* for that word; it means the same or almost the same thing. One definition is an *antonym;* it has the opposite or nearly opposite meaning. The other has a completely different meaning. Label the definitions S for *synonym*, A for *antonym*, and D for *different*.

   _____ a. vegetables

   _____ b. create

   _____ c. destroy

2. **Distinguishing Fact from Opinion**

   Two of the statements below present *facts*, which can be proved correct. The other statement is an *opinion*, which expresses someone's thoughts or beliefs. Label the statements F for *fact* and O for *opinion*.

   _____ a. In the first century A.D., Hero of Alexandria invented a working steam engine.

   _____ b. Hero of Alexandria invented many different things.

   _____ c. Hero of Alexandria was the most brilliant engineer of all time.

19

3. Keeping Events in Order

Label the statements below 1, 2, and 3 to show the order in which the events happened.

_____ a. Hero of Alexandria invented a working steam engine.

_____ b. Dr. Landels estimated that Hero's steam engine was only about one percent efficient.

_____ c. A British professor built a working model of Hero's steam engine.

4. Making Correct Inferences

Two of the statements below are correct *inferences,* or reasonable guesses. They are based on information in the passage. The other statement is an incorrect, or faulty, inference. Label the statements C for *correct* inference and F for *faulty* inference.

_____ a. Everything invented in modern times had probably already been invented long ago.

_____ b. Many discoveries are really rediscoveries of things known to the world in ancient times.

_____ c. To be practical for use, a machine should be efficient.

5. Understanding Main Ideas

One of the statements below expresses the main idea of the passage. One statement is too general, or too broad. The other explains only part of the passage; it is too narrow. Label the statements M for *main idea,* B for *too broad,* and N for *too narrow.*

_____ a. The world's first steam engine was invented by Hero of Alexandria in the first century A.D., but it was too inefficient to be practical.

_____ b. Hero of Alexandria was one of the most inventive people who ever lived.

_____ c. Dr. J. G. Landels wanted to find out whether Hero's steam engine might have had a practical use.

Correct Answers, Part A _____

Correct Answers, Part B _____

Total Correct Answers _____

In ancient Greece, festival days were holidays for everyone. There were 70 festival days in the year. Every four years, a festival was held to honor the goddess Athena. It lasted from six to nine days. The festival opened with games and athletic contests. One contest featured a race with lighted torches. The torch race was a relay race between two teams that passed the torch from runner to runner. The winners of the games received a decorated jar filled with oil from the sacred olive groves. Today people keep up this custom by awarding prize cups to winning teams.

The most famous games in Greece were held in the little town of Olympia. Every four years, runners left Olympia for all parts of the Greek world to announce the start of the games. The games were held in midsummer. Then a sacred truce was declared. If Greeks were at war, they laid down their arms. As a result, people could travel to and from the games safely. Thousands of people headed for Olympia. Servants carried food supplies, cooking equipment, tents, and bedding. Most visitors slept on the floors of the town porches or beneath olive and poplar trees.

The Olympic games were held in honor of Zeus. His gold and ivory image sat enthroned in his Olympic temple. Athletes took an oath to abide by the rules.

The winners were crowned with an olive wreath. Poets wrote about them. Cities held parades for their favorite athletes. Athens gave money prizes to its Olympic champions. Athens also fed winners for the rest of their lives at public expense. At Sparta, Olympic winners had the honor of standing beside the king in battle.

Between athletic events, poets recited their verses to the crowds in the grandstands. Herodotus, the father of history, even read his history of the Persian Wars aloud at the Olympic games. It must have taken him several days of steady reading.

Greek historians dated events by Olympiads. These were the four-year periods when the games were held. The first recorded date in Greek history is 776 B.C., the first Olympiad. This first Olympics had only one event, a short footrace. Over time, the number of events grew to include longer races. The games were held every four years until A.D. 394. Then Greece was ruled by the Roman Empire. The emperor forbade the Olympics as wicked pagan rites.

Reading Time _____

Recalling Facts

1. Games in Olympia were held
   - ❑ a. every summer.
   - ❑ b. once every four years.
   - ❑ c. during the winter.

2. If Greece was at war when the games were scheduled,
   - ❑ a. the games were canceled.
   - ❑ b. a sacred truce was declared.
   - ❑ c. soldiers were not allowed to attend the games.

3. The Olympic games were held in honor of
   - ❑ a. Athena.
   - ❑ b. Venus.
   - ❑ c. Zeus.

4. Olympic winners were
   - ❑ a. appointed as servants to kings.
   - ❑ b. crowned with an olive wreath.
   - ❑ c. elected to public office.

5. Herodotus is known as
   - ❑ a. an Olympic athlete.
   - ❑ b. a Greek god.
   - ❑ c. the father of history.

Understanding Ideas

6. You can conclude from the article that ancient Greeks
   - ❑ a. valued athletic achievement.
   - ❑ b. valued athletic achievement above all else.
   - ❑ c. cared little about athletic achievement.

7. In ancient Greece, the Olympics were
   - ❑ a. poorly attended.
   - ❑ b. popular events.
   - ❑ c. private celebrations.

8. You can conclude that Olympic winners
   - ❑ a. were soon forgotten by their hometowns.
   - ❑ b. received little public attention.
   - ❑ c. became local heroes.

9. You can conclude that the Olympics games were important to the Greeks because
   - ❑ a. wars were temporarily stopped during the games.
   - ❑ b. they were held every four years.
   - ❑ c. poets read their works between events.

10. You can conclude that early Greek athletic contests
    - ❑ a. served as a model for athletic contests today.
    - ❑ b. were wicked pagan rites.
    - ❑ c. drew little attention.

The First Modern Olympics

After the Olympic Games were banned in A.D. 394, no games were held for 1,500 years. In the late 1800s, Baron Pierre de Coubertin of France came up with the idea of reviving the games. Coubertin felt that schools should offer more physical activities. He thought that athletics were an important part of a person's development. Holding Olympic games again might increase interest in athletics.

In 1894, Coubertin presented his idea at an international meeting. People at the meeting liked the idea. They gave it their approval. Before long, a group of organizers from thirteen countries were planning the first modern Olympic Games. Everyone agreed that the games should be held in Greece, where the Olympics began. Two years later in 1896, Greece proudly hosted the first modern Olympics.

At the games, track-and-field events received the most attention. Greece had the largest number of athletes entered in the games. The host country hoped to win some of these events. However, until the marathon, Greece had not won a single track-and-field event.

The marathon would give Greece its first track-and-field victory. Midway through this 25-mile (40-kilometer) race, an American—Arthur Blake—was leading. Then the Greek runner—Spiridon Loues—passed Blake. The crowd cheered as Loues entered the stadium alone. In the excitement, two sons of the Greek king left their seats and ran alongside Loues to the finish line!

1. **Recognizing Words in Context**

   Find the word *held* in the passage. One definition below is a *synonym* for that word; it means the same or almost the same thing. One definition is an *antonym*; it has the opposite or nearly opposite meaning. The other has a completely different meaning. Label the definitions S for *synonym*, A for *antonym*, and D for *different*.

   _____ a. conducted

   _____ b. discontinued

   _____ c. grasped

2. **Distinguishing Fact from Opinion**

   Two of the statements below present *facts*, which can be proved correct. The other statement is an *opinion*, which expresses someone's thoughts or beliefs. Label the statements F for *fact* and O for *opinion*.

   _____ a. Baron Pierre de Coubertin came up with the idea of reviving the Olympic Games.

   _____ b. Schools should offer more physical activities.

   _____ c. No Olympic Games had been held for 1,500 years.

3. Keeping Events in Order

Label the statements below 1, 2, and 3 to show the order in which the events happened.

_____ a. The first modern Olympic Games were held in Greece in 1896.

_____ b. Baron Pierre de Coubertin wanted to revive the Olympic Games.

_____ c. Spiridon Loues won the first modern Olympics marathon.

4. Making Correct Inferences

Two of the statements below are correct *inferences,* or reasonable guesses. They are based on information in the passage. The other statement is an incorrect, or faulty, inference. Label the statements C for *correct* inference and F for *faulty* inference.

_____ a. People around the world were interested in reviving the Olympic Games.

_____ b. Greek athletes were inferior to those from other countries.

_____ c. It was important for Greece to have a winner in the marathon.

5. Understanding Main Ideas

One of the statements below expresses the main idea of the passage. One statement is too general, or too broad. The other explains only part of the passage; it is too narrow. Label the statements M for *main idea*, B for *too broad*, and N for *too narrow*.

_____ a. The Olympic Games have a history dating back more than 2,000 years.

_____ b. The first modern Olympic Games were held in Athens in 1896 through the efforts of Baron Pierre de Coubertin.

_____ c. The sons of the Greek king left their seats and ran to the marathon finish line with Spiridon Loues.

Correct Answers, Part A _____

Correct Answers, Part B _____

Total Correct Answers _____

24

Rain, Snow, and Hail

Far ahead of an approaching storm center, warm, moist air rises and spreads out at high altitudes. As this air mass cools, its moisture condenses and freezes into tiny ice particles, producing cirrus clouds. Often the first sign of a storm is the appearance of these feathery cirrus clouds. Later, as the storm comes closer, these clouds thicken. If the sun or moon is in the sky, an observer might see a halo circling it. This is a fairly reliable sign that it will rain or snow within twenty-four hours.

Later, the clouds become still thicker. They form at lower levels and are made of water droplets rather than ice particles. In the northern temperate zone, winds will then usually shift to the south and blow harder. By this time, rain or snow is usually about six to eight hours away. The south wind becomes steadily stronger, and dark clouds finally appear. Rain or snow usually begins very soon after these clouds are seen.

In the summer, small white clouds that appear in the early morning often turn into dark clouds during the day. Such clouds bring heavy summer showers, with thunder, lightning, and strong, gusty winds. Sometimes, if the clouds push high enough into the very cold upper air, hail will fall.

Rain occurs at temperatures above freezing. The volume of rainfall may be light as in a slight drizzle. Or rainfall may come as a heavy downpour. In some areas, heavy rainfall causes flash flooding. Streams may overflow their banks. Snow will fall at temperatures slightly below freezing.

Hail is balls of ice. The sizes of hailstones may vary. Some may be tiny, the size of a pea or smaller. Others can be the size of baseballs or grapefruit. Hail most often occurs in the spring, and it falls primarily during thunderstorms. Hail begins its descent as rain droplets within a cloud. These droplets are carried upward again and again by strong wind currents to colder regions where they develop several coatings of ice, creating hailstones. When they become too heavy for the cloud to hold, the hailstones fall and pelt the earth. Sleet, or small ice pellets, also begins as rain, but updrafts carry the drops into colder levels of the cloud, causing them to freeze. In Great Britain and parts of the United States, sleet is the name used to describe a mixture of rain and snow.

Reading Time _____

Recalling Facts

1. Cirrus clouds signal
   - ❏ a. fair weather.
   - ❏ b. cool weather.
   - ❏ c. a storm.

2. As a storm nears, moisture in clouds becomes
   - ❏ a. ice particles.
   - ❏ b. fog.
   - ❏ c. water droplets.

3. Snow occurs when the temperature is
   - ❏ a. slightly below freezing.
   - ❏ b. at freezing.
   - ❏ c. slightly above freezing.

4. Hail consists of
   - ❏ a. cold raindrops.
   - ❏ b. invisible ice particles.
   - ❏ c. balls of ice.

5. In the United States, a mixture of rain and snow is known as
   - ❏ a. hail.
   - ❏ b. ice.
   - ❏ c. sleet.

Understanding Ideas

6. When the temperature is above freezing, a storm is likely to produce
   - ❏ a. rain.
   - ❏ b. snow.
   - ❏ c. sleet.

7. To help predict storms, forecasters observe
   - ❏ a. temperature.
   - ❏ b. cloud formations.
   - ❏ c. seasons.

8. Whether it rains, snows, hails, or sleets depends on
   - ❏ a. types of clouds.
   - ❏ b. temperature.
   - ❏ c. the location of the storm center.

9. The main difference between hail and sleet is
   - ❏ a. how they are formed.
   - ❏ b. size.
   - ❏ c. where they are formed.

10. You can conclude from the article that clouds form as a result of
    - ❏ a. moisture in the air.
    - ❏ b. the sun's rays.
    - ❏ c. a halo around the sun or moon.

A Pretty Fair Hurricane

It was raining heavily as Frank and Eleanor pulled out of the mall parking lot. A strong wind bent the tops of trees. "The radio said that there was a hurricane off Cape Hatteras," Eleanor remarked. "Forecasters thought the fringes of it might hit New Jersey."

"That far north? Impossible!" Frank said. He swerved the car to avoid a fallen tree limb. Then just ahead, a large maple tree groaned and fell with a crash, blocking the road. Frank slammed on the car's brakes, and they both gave a sigh of relief that their car was not hit.

"You'd almost think this was the hurricane," Eleanor said.

Another car pulled up behind theirs. Frank got out to talk to the driver. "Looks like we're going to be stuck here awhile," he said as rain dripped down his neck. "Do you suppose this could be a real hurricane?"

The man laughed. "Well, it's pretty windy," he said. "But this is nothing. I've been in real hurricanes in Florida."

The wind whipped rain into their faces. Debris was flying through the air, and another tree came crashing down. The man looked thoughtful. "Maybe it is a hurricane at that," he said finally. "It's not as bad as the hurricanes we get in Florida, but it's a pretty fair one for Connecticut!"

1. Recognizing Words in Context

Find the word *pretty* in the passage. One definition below is a *synonym* for that word; it means the same or almost the same thing. One definition is an *antonym;* it has the opposite or nearly opposite meaning. The other has a completely different meaning. Label the definitions S for *synonym*, A for *antonym*, and D for *different*.

_____ a. attractive

_____ b. somewhat

_____ c. not

2. Distinguishing Fact from Opinion

Two of the statements below present *facts*, which can be proved correct. The other statement is an *opinion*, which expresses someone's thoughts or beliefs. Label the statements F for *fact* and O for *opinion*.

_____ a. A large maple tree fell and blocked the road.

_____ b. The radio said there was a hurricane off Cape Hatteras.

_____ c. It was a pretty fair hurricane for Connecticut.

3. Keeping Events in Order

Two of the statements below describe events that happened at the same time. The other statement describes an event that happened before or after those events. Label them S for *same time,* B for *before,* and A for *after.*

_____ a. Frank talked to the other driver.

_____ b. Rain dripped down Frank's neck.

_____ c. A tree fell and blocked the road.

4. Making Correct Inferences

Two of the statements below are correct *inferences,* or reasonable guesses. They are based on information in the passage. The other statement is an incorrect, or faulty, inference. Label the statements C for *correct* inference and F for *faulty* inference.

_____ a. Hurricanes in Connecticut are never as bad as hurricanes in Florida.

_____ b. It really was a hurricane.

_____ c. Hurricanes are not common in Connecticut.

5. Understanding Main Ideas

One of the statements below expresses the main idea of the passage. One statement is too general, or too broad. The other explains only part of the passage; it is too narrow. Label the statements M for *main idea,* B for *too broad,* and N for *too narrow.*

_____ a. Hurricanes are destructive, deadly storms.

_____ b. Frank and Eleanor were caught in a storm that may have been a hurricane.

_____ c. Debris was flying through the air.

Correct Answers, Part A _____

Correct Answers, Part B _____

Total Correct Answers _____

Many animals that live in water are called fishes. A fish is a water-dwelling, cold-blooded animal that has a backbone and breathes by means of gills. It normally has two pairs of fins instead of arms and legs, as well as several other fins. Many fishes are covered with scales. More than 20,000 living kinds of fishes are known, and new species are discovered every year. This is more than all the other kinds of backboned animals combined.

Other animals also live in the water at least part of the time. They, too, have backbones and early in life breathe underwater by means of gills. These are the amphibians—primarily frogs, toads, and salamanders.

How can one tell fishes from amphibians? Fishes have fins as appendages, and most have scales that cover the body. Most adult amphibians have legs and no body scales. Fishes never have true legs. The scales of a fish overlap each other like shingles on a roof. The scales are not shed like the hair or feathers of mammals and birds. But if any are lost by accident, new ones grow to take their place.

The most highly developed fishes are those with a bony skeleton. They are also the most abundant and familiar. The mackerel is typical of this highest order of fishes. Observing how easily and swiftly fishes cut the water, people pattern boats and submarines after their streamlined bodies. A typical fish is spindle-shaped but somewhat wider in front of the middle. The head joins the body without a neck. The eyes are flush with the head; the gill openings are covered with a smooth flap. Only the fins extend beyond the body, and they can be pressed flat against the sides. These features help the fish move smoothly through the water. Water resistance is further lessened by a coating of slime.

Unlike human beings, most fishes continue to grow as long as they live. Old fish may become very large. The exceptions are fish such as the salmon, which have a definite period of growth before spawning and, after spawning, die. Carp are said to have a life span of 100 years, but few fish in the wild die of old age. Though many fishes are believed to reach ages of 50 to 100 years, scientific documentation for individuals reaching ages beyond 15 to 20 years in natural environments is rare.

Reading Time _____

Recalling Facts

1. Fishes breathe by means of
   - ❏ a. noses.
   - ❏ b. lungs.
   - ❏ c. gills.

2. Fishes never have
   - ❏ a. legs.
   - ❏ b. tails.
   - ❏ c. fins.

3. The most highly developed fishes are
   - ❏ a. amphibians.
   - ❏ b. those with bony skeletons.
   - ❏ c. those with scales.

4. Most fishes differ from humans in that they
   - ❏ a. stop growing when they reach adulthood.
   - ❏ b. reach their full growth in infancy.
   - ❏ c. continue to grow as long as they live.

5. An example of an amphibian is the
   - ❏ a. salamander.
   - ❏ b. carp.
   - ❏ c. mackerel.

Understanding Ideas

6. Fish, like humans,
   - ❏ a. have gills.
   - ❏ b. have backbones.
   - ❏ c. live underwater.

7. You can conclude from the article that the fastest boats are those that
   - ❏ a. are covered with slime.
   - ❏ b. are wide in the middle.
   - ❏ c. offer the least water resistance.

8. In terms of growth and life span, salmon are
   - ❏ a. typical of most fish.
   - ❏ b. different from most other fish.
   - ❏ c. the animals most like human beings.

9. It is likely that the number of known species of fish will
   - ❏ a. decrease in the future.
   - ❏ b. increase in the future.
   - ❏ c. stay the same.

10. You can conclude that fish in captivity are
    - ❏ a. less likely to die from old age.
    - ❏ b. more likely to die from old age.
    - ❏ c. more likely to die from disease.

5 B The Thirsty Moose

AN ABENAKI TALE

Long ago, the Merrimack River flowed straight and smooth through the countryside. There were so many salmon, shad, and eels in its water that the people used the fish to fertilize their fields.

One spring, a giant moose made its way down to the river and began to drink. The thirsty moose drank and drank and drank. It swallowed so much water that the fish became worried. They feared that it would drink the river dry!

One wise old fish knew what to do. The fish whispered to a blackfly, and the blackfly flew onto the moose's nose and bit it! Bellowing in pain, the moose threw back its great head. It began stamping the ground with its huge hooves. It stamped so hard that it broke the flat land into the rocky steps of a stairway! The river that had flowed so smoothly was now sent headlong down a series of waterfalls. The river ran away from the moose so swiftly that the moose could no longer endanger it. As swiftly as the river ran away from it, the moose ran away from the raging current.

Finally, the river and its fish were safe from the thirsty moose. The people named the new waterfalls Namoskeag, "the place where one finds small fish."

1. **Recognizing Words in Context**

   Find the word *safe* in the passage. One definition below is a *synonym* for that word; it means the same or almost the same thing. One definition is an *antonym;* it has the opposite or nearly opposite meaning. The other has a completely different meaning. Label the definitions S for *synonym,* A for *antonym,* and D for *different.*

   _____ a. protected

   _____ b. endangered

   _____ c. harmless

2. **Distinguishing Fact from Opinion**

   Two of the statements below present *facts,* which can be proved correct. The other statement is an *opinion,* which expresses someone's thoughts or beliefs. Label the statements F for *fact* and O for *opinion.*

   _____ a. There were so many fish in the river that the people used them to fertilize their fields.

   _____ b. The Abenakis made up interesting tales.

   _____ c. The people named the falls Namoskeag.

3. Keeping Events in Order

Label the statements below 1, 2, and 3 to show the order in which the events happened.

_____ a. A blackfly bit the moose on the nose.

_____ b. The moose stamped the ground with its huge hooves.

_____ c. The flat land was broken into rocky steps.

4. Making Correct Inferences

Two of the statements below are correct *inferences,* or reasonable guesses. They are based on information in the passage. The other statement is an incorrect, or faulty, inference. Label the statements C for *correct* inference and F for *faulty* inference.

_____ a. This is a true story about how the falls were created.

_____ b. The Abenakis made up this tale to explain how the falls were created.

_____ c. The bite of a blackfly is painful.

5. Understanding Main Ideas

One of the statements below expresses the main idea of the passage. One statement is too general, or too broad. The other explains only part of the passage; it is too narrow. Label the statements M for *main idea,* B for *too broad,* and N for *too narrow.*

_____ a. An Abenaki tale explains how the Namoskeag Falls were created by the stamping hooves of a giant moose.

_____ b. A wise old fish whispered to a blackfly.

_____ c. Legends that explain how something came to be are called "porquoi" tales.

Correct Answers, Part A _____

Correct Answers, Part B _____

Total Correct Answers _____

Everyday Life in Ancient Egypt

People today live in an age when every year brings forth new inventions and discoveries and new fads and fashions that affect everyday life. Through communications, migration, and travel, every culture can merge into new life-styles.

The ancient Egyptians had their greatest creative period at the beginning of their long history. After that, their way of living changed very little through the years. It is therefore possible to describe their home life and their art without reference to the different periods of ancient Egyptian history.

Of all the early peoples, the Egyptians were the least warlike. Their country was protected by the sea on the north and by deserts to the east and west. For many centuries, they could develop their own way of life without fear of invasion by foreign armies.

Most villages and towns were situated near the Nile because it was the chief highway and only source of water. Even the rich lived in mud-brick houses. Windows were small, high openings covered with loosely woven matting to keep out the heat and glare of the sun. The most fashionable district was near the king's palace. Even here, houses were crowded close together to leave more space for farmland. Some dwellings were two stories high. Some opened onto a narrow street; others faced a small walled garden.

The ancient Egyptians stored their water and food in huge pottery jars. To prepare foods, the cook used pottery bowls, placing them directly on the fire or in a clay oven. The cook baked bread and cake and roasted beef, mutton, goose, and wildfowl. The common drinks were beer, wine, and milk. Honey and dates were the only sweets.

The members of Egypt's upper classes spent much of their time tending to their appearance. Men shaved with a bronze razor. They cut their hair short and wore wigs. Women also wore wigs or added false braids to their own hair. They had combs and hairpins and mirrors of polished bronze or silver.

Because of the hot climate, both men and women wore white linen clothes. Men usually wore only a skirt. In the early centuries, the skirts were short and narrow. Later they were long and full. Women wore low-cut white dresses with bands over the shoulders. Both men and women wore jewelry collars and necklaces, strings of beads, bracelets, anklets, earrings, and finger rings. Silver was more precious than gold.

Reading Time _____

Recalling Facts

1. The Egyptians were most creative
   - ❏ a. at the beginning of their history.
   - ❏ b. during the middle years of their history.
   - ❏ c. at the end of their history.

2. Egypt is bordered on three sides by
   - ❏ a. water.
   - ❏ b. desert.
   - ❏ c. the sea and deserts.

3. The only source of water for Egyptians was
   - ❏ a. the sea.
   - ❏ b. underground wells.
   - ❏ c. the Nile.

4. The most valued metal for jewelry in ancient Egypt was
   - ❏ a. silver.
   - ❏ b. gold.
   - ❏ c. bronze.

5. Cooking utensils were made of
   - ❏ a. metal.
   - ❏ b. stone.
   - ❏ c. pottery.

Understanding Ideas

6. Regarding their appearance, upper-class Egyptians could be considered
   - ❏ a. vain.
   - ❏ b. modest.
   - ❏ c. casual.

7. You can conclude from the article that the Nile was
   - ❏ a. a large, paved road.
   - ❏ b. an inland waterway.
   - ❏ c. Egypt's only street.

8. It is likely that the Egyptian life-style changed very little because of
   - ❏ a. a lack of foreign influence.
   - ❏ b. the hot weather.
   - ❏ c. boredom.

9. Silver was more precious than gold probably because it was
   - ❏ a. easier to find.
   - ❏ b. scarcer.
   - ❏ c. easier to shape.

10. The Egyptians' concern for personal appearance is suggested by their wearing of
    - ❏ a. white linen.
    - ❏ b. skirts.
    - ❏ c. jewelry.

Simut stood outside his home, deep within the Valley of the Kings. Simut was one of the many skilled artisans and artists living in his village. They earned their living decorating the elaborate tombs of Egypt's pharaohs and queens.

"Ho, Simut," called his friend Pashed. Simut joined Pashed and the other workers. They hiked over the mountain to one of the royal tombs that was under construction. For eight days, they would live in small huts on the mountainside, close to the work site. After eight days of work, they would return home to their families for two days of rest.

The great tombs were built by thousands. Architects, engineers, stonecutters, stonemasons, artists, sculptors, and others workers planned, built, and decorated the tombs. The stonemasons spent long hours carving underground passages and rooms out of the mountain of stone. After them came the plasterers, who created smooth, white walls. Then it was the turn of Simut and other artists and artisans. Following the plans for the large paintings that would cover the tomb's walls, Simut transferred the drawings to the plaster. When Simut completed the outlines, other artists filled them in with brilliant colors. The pictures showed scenes of everyday life and of guides to the afterlife. Thousands of years later, archaeologists would discover and admire the work of Simut and his fellow artists.

1. **Recognizing Words in Context**

   Find the word *brilliant* in the passage. One definition below is a *synonym* for that word; it means the same or almost the same thing. One definition is an *antonym;* it has the opposite or nearly opposite meaning. The other has a completely different meaning. Label the definitions S for *synonym,* A for *antonym,* and D for *different.*

   _____ a. dull

   _____ b. intelligent

   _____ c. bright

2. **Distinguishing Fact from Opinion**

   Two of the statements below present *facts,* which can be proved correct. The other statement is an *opinion,* which expresses someone's thoughts or beliefs. Label the statements F for *fact* and O for *opinion.*

   _____ a. Artists first drew outlines for the paintings, then filled them in with colors.

   _____ b. Tomb workers spent eight days at a time away from home while working on a tomb.

   _____ c. The artists of ancient Egypt were the most skilled artisans in the world.

3. Keeping Events in Order

Label the statements below 1, 2, and 3 to show the order in which the events happened.

_____ a. Plasterers made the tomb walls smooth and white.

_____ b. Artists drew pictures on the tomb walls.

_____ c. Stonemasons carved the underground passages and rooms.

4. Making Correct Inferences

Two of the statements below are correct *inferences,* or reasonable guesses. They are based on information in the passage. The other statement is an incorrect, or faulty, inference. Label the statements C for *correct* inference and F for *faulty* inference.

_____ a. Archaeologists know the names of the workers who constructed and decorated Egyptian tombs.

_____ b. The labor of many different workers was required to create a pharaoh's tomb.

_____ c. Villages were created just for the tomb workers and their families.

5. Understanding Main Ideas

One of the statements below expresses the main idea of the passage. One statement is too general, or too broad. The other explains only part of the passage; it is too narrow. Label the statements M for *main idea,* B for *too broad,* and N for *too narrow.*

_____ a. By studying the tombs of ancient Egyptian pharaohs, archaeologists have learned about the daily lives of these people.

_____ b. Simut lived in the Valley of the Kings.

_____ c. Simut, an Egyptian artist, drew the outlines of paintings on tomb walls.

Correct Answers, Part A _____

Correct Answers, Part B _____

Total Correct Answers _____

Certain varieties of plums have such firm flesh and high sugar content that they can be dried with little loss of their original plumpness and flavor. These plums are called prune plums, and the dried plums themselves are called prunes.

It is believed that the ancient peoples of the Middle East were the first to dry plums to make prunes. Prunes have been prepared for centuries in France, and the prunes from the region around Agen are still considered to be the best in the world. Today, orchards in California, which use Agen plums almost exclusively, yield a major share of the world's prunes. Other prune-growing states include Oregon and Washington. Prunes are also produced in some central European and South American countries.

Prune plums are harvested by machine or gathered from the ground after they have become so ripe that they can be shaken from the trees. The plums selected for drying are washed in hot water or in a weak lye solution to remove bloom, a powdery coating, and dirt from the skins. Next, they are placed in trays and are dried in the sun or in artificially heated dehydrators. Almost all prunes are dried with the pit intact, though the French Brignolles prune is pitted and peeled before drying. Sun drying may take as long as two weeks; dehydration usually takes no longer than 24 hours. Underdried prunes are removed, and the satisfactory ones are placed in bins for curing for two to three weeks or longer. This process softens the skins hardened by drying and gives the prunes a uniform moisture content.

After curing, the prunes are taken to packing plants. Here they are inspected and graded according to size. Large prunes range from 20 to 30 to the pound (0.454 kilogram); there may be as many as 100 smaller prunes per pound (0.454 kilogram). Next, the prunes are treated with hot water or steam to sterilize their skins. Finally, they are packed in cardboard cartons or wooden boxes. The choicest are packed like dates and are eaten without cooking.

Prunes are a good source of vitamins A and B; are high in fiber; and are rich in iron, calcium, and phosphorus. Their pulp is used as food for infants. Prunes are eaten raw, soaked or stewed alone or with other fruits, and used in jams and desserts. The pulp, stewed fruit, and juice are packaged commercially.

Reading Time _____

Recalling Facts

1. Prunes are
   - ❏ a. fresh plums.
   - ❏ b. unripe plums.
   - ❏ c. dried plums.

2. The world's best prunes come from
   - ❏ a. a region in France.
   - ❏ b. Oregon.
   - ❏ c. the Middle East.

3. A prune's powdery coating is called
   - ❏ a. fur.
   - ❏ b. bloom.
   - ❏ c. skin.

4. Curing prunes results in
   - ❏ a. hard skins.
   - ❏ b. uniform moisture content.
   - ❏ c. dehydration.

5. Prunes are a good source of
   - ❏ a. fiber.
   - ❏ b. protein.
   - ❏ c. vitamin C.

Understanding Ideas

6. You can conclude from the article that prunes
   - ❏ a. have little nutritional value.
   - ❏ b. are low in sugar.
   - ❏ c. are considered a healthy food.

7. It is likely that ancient people dried prunes
   - ❏ a. in the sun.
   - ❏ b. using salt water.
   - ❏ c. in heated dehydrators.

8. You can conclude that prune packagers are concerned about
   - ❏ a. how to remove prune pits.
   - ❏ b. how to package small prunes.
   - ❏ c. germs on prune skins.

9. You can conclude that the best prunes are made from plums that are
   - ❏ a. fully ripe.
   - ❏ b. green.
   - ❏ c. not quite ripe.

10. You can conclude that prunes processed in less than three weeks are
    - ❏ a. dried in dehydrators.
    - ❏ b. inferior in quality.
    - ❏ c. dried in the sun.

Promoting Prunes

"Wow! I didn't realize how good prunes are for you," Nita remarked at breakfast. She held up a box of prunes. "Listen to this: 'High in fiber. Rich in iron and calcium. Rich in vitamins A and B.' This gives me an idea for the Health Fair!"

"What's your idea?" her brother Rico asked.

"Well, you know how no one seems to like prunes. I mean, maybe your mother makes you eat them." Nita glanced at her mother, who was reading the newspaper. "But did you ever eat one just because you wanted a prune?"

"No, I can't say that they are my first choice for a snack or dessert," Rico admitted.

"So I'm going to create a campaign to make prunes popular!" said Nita. "Bumper stickers, buttons, posters—the works! I'll have to come up with a catchy slogan."

"Prunes—good and good for you," suggested Rico. "Or—Got prunes?"

By the time they left for school, Nita had filled a pad with slogan ideas. In her health class, she talked two friends into working with her on the project. On Health Fair day, they were all set. Everyone applauded as they danced into the gym dressed as prunes singing to the tune of a familiar commercial: "Oh, I wish I were a California prune."

1. **Recognizing Words in Context**

   Find the word *rich* in the passage. One definition below is a *synonym* for that word; it means the same or almost the same thing. One definition is an *antonym;* it has the opposite or nearly opposite meaning. The other has a completely different meaning. Label the definitions S for *synonym*, A for *antonym,* and D for *different*.

   _____ a. nutrient-filled

   _____ b. lacking

   _____ c. wealthy

2. **Distinguishing Fact from Opinion**

   Two of the statements below present *facts,* which can be proved correct. The other statement is an *opinion,* which expresses someone's thoughts or beliefs. Label the statements F for *fact* and O for *opinion.*

   _____ a. Prunes are rich in iron and calcium.

   _____ b. Prunes are high in fiber.

   _____ c. No one seems to like prunes.

3. Keeping Events in Order

Two of the statements below describe events that happened at the same time. The other statement describes an event that happened before or after those events. Label them S for *same time*, B for *before*, and A for *after*.

_____ a. Nita and her friends danced into the gym dressed as prunes.

_____ b. Nita came up with an idea for the Health Fair.

_____ c. Everyone applauded.

4. Making Correct Inferences

Two of the statements below are correct *inferences*, or reasonable guesses. They are based on information in the passage. The other statement is an incorrect, or faulty, inference. Label the statements C for *correct* inference and F for *faulty* inference.

_____ a. Prunes are a healthful food.

_____ b. People attending the Health Fair enjoyed Nita and her friends' performance.

_____ c. Because of Nita's Health Fair project, people in her school began eating more prunes.

5. Understanding Main Ideas

One of the statements below expresses the main idea of the passage. One statement is too general, or too broad. The other explains only part of the passage; it is too narrow. Label the statements M for *main idea*, B for *too broad*, and N for *too narrow*.

_____ a. Everyone applauded as Nita and her friends danced into the gym dressed as prunes and singing.

_____ b. Prunes are delicious and good for you.

_____ c. A box of prunes gave Nita the idea of promoting prunes as a Health Fair project, which she carried out with the help of friends.

Correct Answers, Part A _____

Correct Answers, Part B _____

Total Correct Answers _____

The Basics of Bicycling

Bicycling is a simple activity that people of all ages can enjoy. However, pedaling, braking, and shifting gears correctly can improve the fun and efficiency of cycling.

On any bike, the way a rider pedals will affect the quality of the ride. The rider should make sure the bike seat, or saddle, is properly adjusted. It should be high enough so that the rider's leg is almost fully extended while his or her heel is on the pedal. Toe clips can help make pedal action easier. They allow for a strong downward stroke and an upward thrust.

The best way to achieve smooth, strong pedaling is to practice on low to moderate gears. Most beginners pedal at a rate of only 50 to 60 revolutions per minute (rpm). At 70 to 90 rpm, riders approach peak efficiency and can pedal for hours without strain. Pedaling too long in high gears can cause fatigue and muscle cramps and hurt the knees.

On many bikes, riders shift gears to maintain pedaling speed. A typical 10-speed bike has two sizes of chainwheels in front and five gears, or sprockets, in the rear. This combination provides ten speeds. For flat, open-road riding, a middle gear works best. In middle gear, the chain is on the large chainwheel in front and the middle sprocket in the rear. For climbing hills, a rider should use lower gears in which the chain is on a smaller chainwheel in front and a bigger gear in the rear. For riding downhill or with tailwinds, the rider should shift to a higher gear, which uses the larger chainwheel and a smaller sprocket.

Bicycles have brakes for stopping. One-speed bikes have coaster brakes, which a rider operates by pedaling backward. Multispeed bikes have hand brakes. Hand brakes may cause the wheels to lock if their levers are squeezed too hard. A rider should brake by squeezing and then releasing the brake levers in rhythm. On a 10-speed bike, the front wheel supports most of the rider's weight and has the best traction. A rider should use the front brake first. Next, he or she should apply both brakes until the rear wheel locks and then immediately ease the pressure on the rear brake. This will permit that wheel to roll. Then the rider applies the brakes again.

Together, rhythmic braking, proper gear use, and even pedaling can make bicycling more enjoyable.

Reading Time _____

Recalling Facts

1. The way a bike is pedaled affects
   - ❑ a. the height of the seat.
   - ❑ b. the quality of the ride.
   - ❑ c. how well it steers.

2. Pedaling too long in high gears can cause
   - ❑ a. muscle cramps.
   - ❑ b. poor traction.
   - ❑ c. gear stripping.

3. Peak pedaling efficiency is achieved when a rider pedals
   - ❑ a. 50 to 60 revolutions per minute.
   - ❑ b. 70 to 90 revolutions per minute.
   - ❑ c. 100 to 110 revolutions per minute.

4. Brakes on multispeed bikes are
   - ❑ a. hand brakes.
   - ❑ b. coaster brakes.
   - ❑ c. foot brakes.

5. Gears are shifted in order to
   - ❑ a. maintain pedaling speed.
   - ❑ b. reduce braking.
   - ❑ c. keep wheels rolling.

Understanding Ideas

6. A better-quality ride is achieved by
   - ❑ a. beginning bike riders.
   - ❑ b. riders who have practiced biking techniques.
   - ❑ c. pedaling as fast as possible.

7. Efficient pedaling is the result of
   - ❑ a. wearing toe clips.
   - ❑ b. pushing downward without strain.
   - ❑ c. a strong downward stroke and an upward thrust.

8. Bikers traveling long distances should use
   - ❑ a. high gears.
   - ❑ b. low to moderate gears.
   - ❑ c. rear wheel locks.

9. The distance between the seat and the pedal should depend on
   - ❑ a. how fast a rider pedals.
   - ❑ b. the style of the bike.
   - ❑ c. the length of the rider's leg.

10. You can conclude from the article that compared to one-speed bikes, multispeed bikes are
    - ❑ a. easier to learn to ride.
    - ❑ b. harder to pedal.
    - ❑ c. more efficient.

"Ready to get going?" Mike Hale asked. He and his two children were heading home from a two-week camping trip in the Idaho wilderness.

"Ready, Dad," said Kim. She hauled her backpack over to her bike, followed by her brother, Greg. Their bikes stood upright on one rail of an abandoned railroad track. Once again, Kim had to admire her father's cleverness. He had designed these special bikes, which he called railcycles. He had gotten the idea from a velocipede—a pedal-powered vehicle that railroad workers once rode while inspecting tracks.

Each bike had four small wheels ahead of the front wheel. These guided the bike as it rolled along the rail. A metal bar called an outrigger stretched from the bike to the other rail. The outrigger helped steady the bike and held supplies. Kim and her brother attached their backpacks, sleeping bags, and tents to the bar. Then they mounted the bikes and were off.

"What a great way to see the country!" Greg shouted over his shoulder. "Next year, I want to go to Montana, Dad."

"I'll find out about abandoned railroad lines there," Mike said. "We want to be sure there's no chance of running into a train. That would be too much of an adventure!"

1. Recognizing Words in Context

Find the word *steady* in the passage. One definition below is a *synonym* for that word; it means the same or almost the same thing. One definition is an *antonym;* it has the opposite or nearly opposite meaning. The other has a completely different meaning. Label the definitions S for *synonym,* A for *antonym,* and D for *different.*

_____ a. constant

_____ b. weaken

_____ c. brace

2. Distinguishing Fact from Opinion

Two of the statements below present *facts,* which can be proved correct. The other statement is an *opinion,* which expresses someone's thoughts or beliefs. Label the statements F for *fact* and O for *opinion.*

_____ a. Four small wheels are attached ahead of the bike's front wheel.

_____ b. Mr. Hale got the idea for railcycles from vehicles used by railroad workers.

_____ c. Riding railcycles is a great way to see the country.

3. Keeping Events in Order

Two of the statements below describe events that happened at the same time. The other statement describes an event that happened before or after those events. Label them S for *same time,* B for *before,* and A for *after.*

_____ a. Kim hauled her backpack to her bike.

_____ b. Kim and Greg attached their backpacks to the outrigger.

_____ c. Greg followed Kim.

4. Making Correct Inferences

Two of the statements below are correct *inferences,* or reasonable guesses. They are based on information in the passage. The other statement is an incorrect, or faulty, inference. Label the statements C for *correct* inference and F for *faulty* inference.

_____ a. Mr. Hale had checked before the trip to be sure the tracks they were riding on were abandoned.

_____ b. It is safe to use a railcycle on any railroad tracks.

_____ c. The Hales enjoy taking camping trips on their railcycles.

5. Understanding Main Ideas

One of the statements below expresses the main idea of the passage. One statement is too general, or too broad. The other explains only part of the passage; it is too narrow. Label the statements M for *main idea,* B for *too broad,* and N for *too narrow.*

_____ a. When it comes to planet-friendly modes of transportation, it is hard to beat a bicycle.

_____ b. An outrigger bar helps hold the railcycle steady.

_____ c. The Hale family takes trips on specially designed bicycles that ride on rails.

Correct Answers, Part A _____

Correct Answers, Part B _____

Total Correct Answers _____

44

Floating icebergs are at once the dread of sailors and the wonder of all who see them for the first time. They are the broken-off ends of glaciers that slide into the sea. Some are small and flat. Others form mountains of ice a mile (1.6 kilometers) or more across and more than 200 feet (61 meters) above the water.

Hiding beneath the sea is the largest part of an iceberg. This part is about seven times as large as the part above. This is because an iceberg is made of freshwater ice, which weighs about seven-eighths as much as seawater. In freshwater, an iceberg would sink down until about nine-tenths was below the surface.

These wanderers of the sea are often surrounded by fog. On clear days, they shimmer in the sun with dazzling beauty, reflecting the tints of sea and sky. As they drift, many take on the shapes of castles, arches, and domes. At night, the bergs glow with an odd whiteness called blink. Blink is the reflection of weak light rays from the crystal surface.

New icebergs are being formed all the time. Most of those in the north Atlantic break off from the fringes of Greenland's great icecap. Here in the early spring thaws, a great parade of floating ice islands begins its journey southward. Sometime in April, May, or June, an average of 400 reach the northern Atlantic shipping routes.

Icebergs melt quickly in salt water. High waves and heavy swells rush the process. As they dissolve, icebergs may split in two, roll over, or slough off great fragments with a vast roar. Some bergs, however, are so huge that they travel 2,000 miles (3,200 kilometers) or more before disappearing.

Two shipping routes are especially dangerous: one through the Strait of Belle Isle into the Gulf of St. Lawrence, the other along the Grand Banks. Since 1914, the United States Coast Guard has conducted an ice patrol in the North Atlantic. This service is financed by the maritime nations. Reports of the positions and movements of icebergs are broadcast by radio. The Hydrographic Office issues bulletins that chart the iceberg region. The office also provides charts showing safe "tracks" for shipping. The Coast Guard equips its cutters and planes with radar and loran to fix the location of icebergs. In addition, other sound equipment is lowered into the sea to help locate bergs.

Reading Time _____

Recalling Facts

1. Floating icebergs are
   - ❏ a. mountains of frozen salt water.
   - ❏ b. broken-off ends of glaciers.
   - ❏ c. flat chunks of frozen snow.

2. The ratio of an iceberg's parts that are below to those that are above the water is about
   - ❏ a. two to one.
   - ❏ b. seven to one.
   - ❏ c. twenty to one.

3. The word *blink* refers to
   - ❏ a. the southward journey of icebergs.
   - ❏ b. an iceberg's shape.
   - ❏ c. the white glow of an iceberg at night.

4. Icebergs floating in seawater
   - ❏ a. grow in size.
   - ❏ b. quickly sink.
   - ❏ c. quickly melt.

5. The locations of icebergs are charted using
   - ❏ a. fishing nets.
   - ❏ b. radar and loran.
   - ❏ c. weather balloons.

Understanding Ideas

6. You can conclude from the article that freshwater
   - ❏ a. is more buoyant than salt water.
   - ❏ b. is less buoyant than salt water.
   - ❏ c. has about the same buoyancy as salt water.

7. You can conclude that icebergs present a danger to
   - ❏ a. anything in their path.
   - ❏ b. wildlife.
   - ❏ c. airplanes.

8. The Coast Guard's aim in charting icebergs is to
   - ❏ a. control their course.
   - ❏ b. speed up the melting process.
   - ❏ c. prevent collisions.

9. You can conclude that fixing the location of an iceberg
   - ❏ a. is an ongoing process.
   - ❏ b. prevents it from moving further.
   - ❏ c. is a simple task.

10. It is likely that before the use of modern technology to track icebergs,
    - ❏ a. collisions were a constant danger.
    - ❏ b. ships avoided the North Atlantic.
    - ❏ c. there were few collisions.

Death of the *Titanic*

When it made its maiden voyage in 1912, the *Titanic* was the greatest ship of its time. Nothing had been spared for the comfort of passengers. Below decks, 16 watertight compartments separated by emergency doors made the huge ship unsinkable. At least, that was what the ship's builders thought.

On April 14, the *Titanic*'s officers received disturbing messages from other ships. The Labrador current had carried huge icebergs farther south than usual, well into shipping lanes. The warnings were ignored. Then at 11:40 that night, a young sailor on watch saw something ahead. He rang the lookout bell and sent a message to the bridge: "Iceberg right ahead." Less than a minute later, the ship trembled. Deep down below the water-line, sailors stared unbelievingly as a two-foot-high (60-centimeter-high) rush of icy seawater poured through a gash in the ship's side. An officer hit the lever that closed all the watertight doors. As the sailors climbed an escape ladder, they saw the hull rapidly filling with water.

Just after midnight, the captain ordered the ship abandoned. At 2:20 A.M., those in the lifeboats looking back at the *Titanic* saw the stern of the ship lift clear of the water. Then the *Titanic* slid down into the darkness and was gone. Of more than 2,200 passengers and crew, only 705 survived.

1. **Recognizing Words in Context**

   Find the word *maiden* in the passage. One definition below is a *synonym* for that word; it means the same or almost the same thing. One definition is an *antonym;* it has the opposite or nearly opposite meaning. The other has a completely different meaning. Label the definitions S for *synonym,* A for *antonym,* and D for *different.*

   _____ a. last

   _____ b. first

   _____ c. girl

2. **Distinguishing Fact from Opinion**

   Two of the statements below present *facts,* which can be proved correct. The other statement is an *opinion,* which expresses someone's thoughts or beliefs. Label the statements F for *fact* and O for *opinion.*

   _____ a. The *Titanic* was unsinkable.

   _____ b. The *Titanic* had 16 waterproof compartments separated by emergency doors.

   _____ c. The Labrador current carried huge icebergs into the shipping lanes.

3. Keeping Events in Order

Two of the statements below describe events that happened at the same time. The other statement describes an event that happened before or after those events. Label them S for *same time,* B for *before,* and A for *after.*

_____ a. An officer hit the lever that closed the emergency doors.

_____ b. Sailors climbed an escape ladder.

_____ c. The hull was rapidly filling with water.

4. Making Correct Inferences

Two of the statements below are correct *inferences,* or reasonable guesses. They are based on information in the passage. The other statement is an incorrect, or faulty, inference. Label the statements C for *correct* inference and F for *faulty* inference.

_____ a. Despite the builders' claims, the *Titanic* was not really unsinkable.

_____ b. The iceberg warnings were ignored because no one thought an iceberg could harm the *Titanic.*

_____ c. The iceberg was too close to the ship to be avoided.

5. Understanding Main Ideas

One of the statements below expresses the main idea of the passage. One statement is too general, or too broad. The other explains only part of the passage; it is too narrow. Label the statements M for *main idea,* B for *too broad,* and N for *too narrow.*

_____ a. The *Titanic*'s officers had received messages about icebergs in the shipping lanes.

_____ b. Icebergs pose a hazard to ships.

_____ c. On her maiden voyage, the *Titanic* struck an iceberg and sank.

Correct Answers, Part A _____

Correct Answers, Part B _____

Total Correct Answers _____

Eli Whitney was born just before the American Revolution. He grew up on a farm in New England. There he showed an early ability to repair and make things. As a youth, he helped repair farm tools. He also learned how to make his own nails. At the time, Americans were still purchasing all nails from England. They were very expensive. Once Whitney learned to make nails, he provided his father with all the nails his father needed and also sold them to other people.

Whitney attended Yale University, earning his way partly by repairing tools and furniture. He also made shelves, chests, and tables for other students and professors. After graduation, he accepted a teaching position in Savannah, Georgia, a port city in the cotton-growing South.

Traveling by boat to Georgia, Whitney met Mrs. Nathaniel Greene. She was a widow of a Revolutionary War general and owned a plantation. She liked the young man and took an interest in him. When Whitney arrived in Savannah, he learned that his teaching position was no longer available. He found himself without a job and without money.

Mrs. Greene heard of Whitney's troubles. She asked him to stay on her plantation. To thank her, he began to make things for her household— things that saved work or were convenient.

At that time, cotton was a major crop in the South. Farmers could grow great amounts of cotton. But they could not easily prepare it for market. Cotton seeds had to be removed from the cotton lint by hand. This was very slow work. Textile mills wanted more cotton. The plantation owners could grow it, but they couldn't get the cotton separated from the seeds in large enough quantities to meet demand. They were looking for a way to separate the seeds from the cotton lint more quickly.

Mrs. Greene introduced Whitney to the growers. She thought that he might be able to solve their problem. In just a few short weeks, Whitney built a simple, hand-operated machine that could separate cotton seeds from the lint. The machine could clean many more pounds (kilograms) of lint in a day than a person could by hand. Whitney's invention was the first cotton gin.

Today, thanks to machine-ginning, there is practically no limit to the amount of cotton that can be produced for factory spindles and looms. The growing of cotton has become a huge industry.

Reading Time _____

Recalling Facts

1. Eli Whitney grew up
   - ❏ a. on a southern plantation.
   - ❏ b. on a New England farm.
   - ❏ c. in Savannah, Georgia.

2. Whitney earned his way through Yale by
   - ❏ a. working as a farm laborer.
   - ❏ b. working on a boat.
   - ❏ c. repairing and making furniture.

3. Whitney accepted a teaching position
   - ❏ a. in New England.
   - ❏ b. at Yale.
   - ❏ c. in Savannah, Georgia.

4. Whitney best helped southern plantation owners by making
   - ❏ a. nails.
   - ❏ b. the cotton gin.
   - ❏ c. furniture.

5. The cotton gin
   - ❏ a. helped cotton grow faster.
   - ❏ b. separated cotton from the seeds.
   - ❏ c. made cotton into cloth.

Understanding Ideas

6. A good word to describe Eli Whitney is
   - ❏ a. carefree.
   - ❏ b. shiftless.
   - ❏ c. creative.

7. It is likely that the cotton gin was
   - ❏ a. Whitney's only invention.
   - ❏ b. one of Whitney's most important inventions.
   - ❏ c. one of Whitney's least needed inventions.

8. You can conclude from the article that after the cotton gin was invented,
   - ❏ a. plantation owners grew more cotton.
   - ❏ b. cotton became a major crop in the North.
   - ❏ c. there was less need for cotton.

9. You can conclude that textile mills
   - ❏ a. grow cotton.
   - ❏ b. no longer want cotton.
   - ❏ c. make cotton into cloth.

10. You can conclude that the demand for cotton today
   - ❏ a. continues to be great.
   - ❏ b. cannot keep up with the supply.
   - ❏ c. is declining.

　　　　　After the Cotton Gin

Eli Whitney's cotton gin was a huge success. A worker using Whitney's machine could do the work of fifty people!

You might have thought that Whitney would become rich from sales of his time-saving cotton gin. He thought that himself. Whitney noted, "It is generally said by those who know anything about it, that I shall make a fortune by it." He obtained a patent for the machine. However, not long after he invented it, word about the device spread. Without paying the inventor for his idea, people began making their own cotton gins. The machine brought wealth to the South. To its inventor, however, it brought very little.

Eli Whitney was not discouraged by his failure to make a fortune with the cotton gin. His quick mind was full of ideas. One of his successes was a way to speed up the process of building muskets. Before Eli Whitney came along, the different parts of each musket were made individually. A part from one musket did not fit into the same place in another musket. Whitney developed the idea of uniform, interchangeable musket parts. Whitney bought a factory and made most of the machines needed to build muskets. Pretty soon, he was in the business of making muskets for the government!

1. **Recognizing Words in Context**

   Find the word *uniform* in the passage. One definition below is a *synonym* for that word; it means the same or almost the same thing. One definition is an *antonym;* it has the opposite or nearly opposite meaning. The other has a completely different meaning. Label the definitions S for *synonym,* A for *antonym,* and D for *different.*

   _____ a. unlike

   _____ b. similar

   _____ c. clothes

2. **Distinguishing Fact from Opinion**

   Two of the statements below present *facts,* which can be proved correct. The other statement is an *opinion,* which expresses someone's thoughts or beliefs. Label the statements F for *fact* and O for *opinion.*

   _____ a. People copied Whitney's cotton gin without paying the inventor for his idea.

   _____ b. One person using the cotton gin could do the work of fifty people.

   _____ c. You would have thought that Whitney would become rich from sales of the cotton gin.

3. Keeping Events in Order

Label the statements below 1, 2, and 3 to show the order in which the events happened.

_____ a. Whitney went into business building muskets for the government.

_____ b. People made their own cotton gins using Eli Whitney's idea.

_____ c. Eli Whitney invented the cotton gin.

4. Making Correct Inferences

Two of the statements below are correct *inferences*, or reasonable guesses. They are based on information in the passage. The other statement is an incorrect, or faulty, inference. Label the statements C for *correct* inference and F for *faulty* inference.

_____ a. Eli Whitney was a clever, imaginative person.

_____ b. People did not feel they should pay for a cotton gin when they could make one on their own.

_____ c. Inventors rarely make any money from their ideas.

5. Understanding Main Ideas

One of the statements below expresses the main idea of the passage. One statement is too general, or too broad. The other explains only part of the passage; it is too narrow. Label the statements M for *main idea*, B for *too broad*, and N for *too narrow*.

_____ a. Although he made no money from the cotton gin he invented, Eli Whitney became successful as a manufacturer of muskets.

_____ b. Eli Whitney developed a system of uniform, interchangeable parts for muskets.

_____ c. Eli Whitney was a well-known inventor.

Correct Answers, Part A _____

Correct Answers, Part B _____

Total Correct Answers _____

More than 2,300 years ago, the Greeks used white marble to create the most beautiful temples and statues in the ancient world. The best of these stood upon the Acropolis, a plateau in the heart of Athens. An oblong mass of rock, the Acropolis looks very much like a pedestal. Its almost flat top covers less than eight acres (3.3 hectares).

Perhaps 4,000 years ago, the earliest people of Athens walled in the Acropolis for protection. Here their first kings ruled. Here in later years were the chief shrines of Athena, Greek goddess of war and wisdom. More than 2,500 years ago, the shrines began to rise. Only 90 years later, the Spartans found the Acropolis covered with marble temples and dwellings. They destroyed the dwellings, but they paused in awe and silence before the temples and left them unharmed.

In 480 B.C., the Persians burned or smashed everything on the Acropolis. In 447 B.C., the sculptor Phidias was placed in charge of restoring the Acropolis. Several years before, he had erected a large bronze statue of Athena on the Acropolis. Now he began to build her a shrine. This Doric temple, called the Parthenon (dwelling of the maiden), was opened in 438 B.C.

On the western side of the Parthenon stood statues of Athena and Poseidon, the sea god. Relief carvings studded the outside. Along the portico, between the temple's outside columns and its walls, was a frieze. It extended around the top of the walls. Its images represented the procession that carried a new gown to Athena each year. In the temple was another statue of Athena. Its body was made of ivory and its dress of gold. Its right hand held a statue of Nike, goddess of victory, and its left hand rested upon a shield. A majestic gate was erected at the west end of the Acropolis.

By the 5th century A.D., the Byzantines had made the Parthenon a Christian church. Ten centuries later, the Turks made it a mosque. In 1687, under attack by the Venetians, the Turks stored gunpowder in the mosque. Struck by a cannonball, it exploded, killing 300 people. The roof, walls, and 16 columns lay in ruin.

In 1829, Greece began to redeem the ruins. Some fallen pillars have been restored in the Parthenon, but it is still empty and roofless. It suffered further damage in World War II.

Reading Time _____

Recalling Facts

1. The Acropolis is a
   - ❏ a. white marble statue.
   - ❏ b. small, rocky plateau.
   - ❏ c. Greek temple.

2. The first kings of Athens ruled about
   - ❏ a. 2,000 years ago.
   - ❏ b. 4,000 years ago.
   - ❏ c. 6,000 years ago.

3. The Parthenon was built as a
   - ❏ a. Christian church.
   - ❏ b. palace for a king.
   - ❏ c. shrine to Athena.

4. The Parthenon was destroyed by
   - ❏ a. a cannonball.
   - ❏ b. the Spartans.
   - ❏ c. the effects of time.

5. The Greeks worshipped Nike, goddess of
   - ❏ a. sport.
   - ❏ b. victory.
   - ❏ c. love.

Understanding Ideas

6. You can conclude from the article that Athens was named for the
   - ❏ a. sea god.
   - ❏ b. goddess of victory.
   - ❏ c. goddess of wisdom.

7. It is likely that the Parthenon is still in ruins because
   - ❏ a. Greeks prefer ruins to restored buildings.
   - ❏ b. it cannot be restored.
   - ❏ c. the cost of restoration is great.

8. You can conclude that ancient Greeks
   - ❏ a. cared little for religion.
   - ❏ b. were quite religious.
   - ❏ c. were Christians.

9. The fact that the Greeks used white marble for their temples and statues suggests that
   - ❏ a. white was considered a holy color.
   - ❏ b. no other stone existed.
   - ❏ c. marble was readily available.

10. You can conclude that by the 15th century A.D., Athens
    - ❏ a. was under Greek rule.
    - ❏ b. was controlled by the Turks.
    - ❏ c. had been totally destroyed.

Athena Versus Poseidon

Both Athena and Poseidon wanted to be named protector of the city of Athens. To decide who would receive this honor, the two deities decided to take part in a competition. Each would perform a great deed. Then all the people of Athens would vote to decide the winner.

To show how good a protector he could be, Poseidon struck open the rock of the Acropolis with his trident. Water leaped forth from the cleft in the rock and formed a deep well. Athena touched the earth of the Acropolis gently. From that spot an olive tree—the most prized of all the trees of Greece—grew.

When the vote was put to the people, all the women voted for Athena. All the men voted for Poseidon. Since there were more women than men, Athena won easily. This made Poseidon so angry that he punished the people of Athens by sending a disastrous flood. At the same time, the men decided to take the vote away from the women. From that time on, only men could vote in Athens. Nevertheless, Athena kept her position as protector of the city. To honor her, a large bronze statue of the goddess was erected on the Acropolis.

1. **Recognizing Words in Context**

   Find the word *honor* in the passage. One definition below is a *synonym* for that word; it means the same or almost the same thing. One definition is an *antonym;* it has the opposite or nearly opposite meaning. The other has a completely different meaning. Label the definitions S for *synonym,* A for *antonym,* and D for *different.*

   _____ a. esteem

   _____ b. insult

   _____ c. reputation

2. **Distinguishing Fact from Opinion**

   Two of the statements below present *facts,* which can be proved correct. The other statement is an *opinion,* which expresses someone's thoughts or beliefs. Label the statements F for *fact* and O for *opinion.*

   _____ a. Poseidon's gift to the city was a well.

   _____ b. Athena's gift to the city of Athens was better than Poseidon's gift.

   _____ c. A bronze statue of Athena was erected on the Acropolis.

3. Keeping Events in Order

Two of the statements below describe events that happened at the same time. The other statement describes an event that happened before or after those events. Label them S for *same time*, B for *before*, and A for *after*.

_____ a. Poseidon sent a disastrous flood to punish the Athenians.

_____ b. The women of Athens voted for Athena.

_____ c. The men of Athens took the vote away from the women.

4. Making Correct Inferences

Two of the statements below are correct *inferences*, or reasonable guesses. They are based on information in the passage. The other statement is an incorrect, or faulty, inference. Label the statements C for *correct* inference and F for *faulty* inference.

_____ a. The Greek deities competed against each other for people's respect.

_____ b. Athena and Poseidon really existed.

_____ c. The Athenian men resented the fact that the women held the controlling vote.

5. Understanding Main Ideas

One of the statements below expresses the main idea of the passage. One statement is too general, or too broad. The other explains only part of the passage; it is too narrow. Label the statements M for *main idea*, B for *too broad*, and N for *too narrow*.

_____ a. The ancient Greeks created deities who were responsible for everything in nature.

_____ b. Athena made an olive tree grow on the Acropolis.

_____ c. Athena and Poseidon held a competition to decide which of them would be named protector of Athens.

Correct Answers, Part A _____

Correct Answers, Part B _____

Total Correct Answers _____

To a poet, butterflies and moths are like fluttering flowers. Scientists call this group of insects *Lepidoptera,* a word that means "wings." The wings and certain parts of the bodies of butterflies and moths are covered with fine dust. Under a microscope, one sees that the dust is millions of scales arranged in overlapping rows. Each scale has a tiny stem that fits into a cup-like socket. The beautiful colors and markings of the insect are due to the scales, which come in a remarkable variety of colors.

Butterflies and moths look very much alike. The best way to tell them apart is to examine their antennae, or feelers. Butterfly antennae are slender, and the ends are rounded into little clubs or knobs. Moth antennae lack these knobs. Many of them look like tiny feathers, and some are threadlike.

Most butterflies fly and feed during the daytime. Moths fly at night. Butterflies rest with their wings held upright over their backs, and moths with their wings outspread. These are not safe rules to follow, however, for some moths are lovers of sunshine and some fold their wings.

Different kinds of butterflies and moths live throughout the world. They live in temperate regions, high in snowy mountains, in deserts, and in steamy jungles. They vary in size from the great Atlas moth of India, which is 10 inches (25.5 centimeters) from tip to tip of the spread wings, to the Golden Pygmy of Great Britain, which is only 1/5 inch (0.5 centimeters) across. In North America north of Mexico, there are 8,000 kinds of moths, but only 700 kinds of butterflies.

Like all insects, butterflies and moths have three pairs of legs and a body that is divided into three sections—head, thorax, and abdomen. On the middle section of the body are two pairs of wings. The pair in front is usually the larger. The scales on the wings contain a pigment that gives the insect some of its color.

Certain colors, however, and the iridescent shimmer come from the fine ridges on the scales. The ridges break up the light into the various colors of the spectrum. The beautiful blues, for example, are due to the way in which the light strikes the scales.

These insects feed on the nectar of flowers and on other plant liquids. Soon after they become adult insects, they mate, lay their eggs, and die.

Reading Time _____

Recalling Facts

1. *Lepidoptera* means
   - ❏ a. butterfly.
   - ❏ b. wings.
   - ❏ c. scales.

2. The dust on butterflies and moths is made up of
   - ❏ a. dirt particles.
   - ❏ b. feathers.
   - ❏ c. scales.

3. The best way to tell the difference between butterflies and moths is to study their
   - ❏ a. antennae.
   - ❏ b. wings.
   - ❏ c. bodies.

4. The largest moth is found in
   - ❏ a. North America.
   - ❏ b. India.
   - ❏ c. Great Britain.

5. Some of the colors on a butterfly's wings come from
   - ❏ a. a pigment contained in the scales.
   - ❏ b. the nectar of flowers.
   - ❏ c. the effect of light on moisture in the air.

Understanding Ideas

6. It is likely that a member of the *Lepidoptera* family seen flying during the day is
   - ❏ a. a butterfly.
   - ❏ b. a moth.
   - ❏ c. another kind of winged insect.

7. You can conclude from the article butterflies and moths
   - ❏ a. prefer temperate climates.
   - ❏ b. have adapted to many different environments.
   - ❏ c. live only in dry environments.

8. The article suggests that the coloring on butterflies and moths is
   - ❏ a. likely to fade.
   - ❏ b. typical of most insects.
   - ❏ c. unusual.

9. You can conclude that the *Lepidoptera* group of insects
   - ❏ a. is completely unlike other insects.
   - ❏ b. has some characteristics in common with other insects.
   - ❏ c. is exactly like other insects.

10. You can conclude that butterflies and moths live
    - ❏ a. for many years.
    - ❏ b. longer than most insects.
    - ❏ c. only long enough to reproduce.

What was eating the parsley? There it was—a handsome, fat green caterpillar with black bands spotted with yellow. Mai wondered what kind of butterfly it would become. She found an old fish tank. In it she put the caterpillar, a branched stick, and a handful of parsley. She covered the tank with a screen. The caterpillar quickly began munching the parsley.

A few days later the caterpillar climbed the stick. Clinging with its lower feet, it spun a fine silken thread that it looped around its upper body like a sling. Leaning back, the caterpillar began to wriggle. Its skin split and fell away. The new skin underneath hardened into a colorful, hard-shelled chrysalis.

One day Mai noticed that the chrysalis was becoming transparent. As she watched, the chrysalis began to move. Suddenly it split, and a butterfly pulled itself out. It grasped the stick with long, slender legs. Its tiny, wet wings were black, edged with orange and blue spots. The butterfly began to pulse rhythmically, and its wings expanded. Mai identified it as an eastern black swallowtail. She carried the butterfly outside on the stick. It continued to cling to the stick, waving its wings gently in the air. While Mai watched, the swallowtail fluttered up and away.

1. **Recognizing Words in Context**

    Find the word *split* in the passage. One definition below is a *synonym* for that word; it means the same or almost the same thing. One definition is an *antonym;* it has the opposite or nearly opposite meaning. The other has a completely different meaning. Label the definitions S for *synonym*, A for *antonym,* and D for *different*.

    _____ a. shared

    _____ b. divided

    _____ c. joined

2. **Distinguishing Fact from Opinion**

    Two of the statements below present *facts,* which can be proved correct. The other statement is an *opinion,* which expresses someone's thoughts or beliefs. Label the statements F for *fact* and O for *opinion.*

    _____ a. The caterpillar ate parsley.

    _____ b. The caterpillar became a swallowtail butterfly.

    _____ c. The caterpillar was handsome.

3. Keeping Events in Order

Label the statements below 1, 2, and 3 to show the order in which the events happened.

_____ a. The chrysalis became transparent.

_____ b. The caterpillar shed its skin.

_____ c. A butterfly emerged from the chrysalis.

4. Making Correct Inferences

Two of the statements below are correct *inferences,* or reasonable guesses. They are based on information in the passage. The other statement is an incorrect, or faulty, inference. Label the statements C for *correct* inference and F for *faulty* inference.

_____ a. A butterfly develops inside a chrysalis.

_____ b. Caterpillars make good pets.

_____ c. Mai was interested in observing nature.

5. Understanding Main Ideas

One of the statements below expresses the main idea of the passage. One statement is too general, or too broad. The other explains only part of the passage; it is too narrow. Label the statements M for *main idea,* B for *too broad,* and N for *too narrow.*

_____ a. The chrysalis became transparent and split open, and a butterfly emerged.

_____ b. Mai observes as a caterpillar becomes first a chrysalis and then a butterfly.

_____ c. Butterflies undergo several changes over the course of their life cycle.

Correct Answers, Part A _____

Correct Answers, Part B _____

Total Correct Answers _____

John Paul Jones

The first great American naval hero was Captain John Paul Jones. A strong, resourceful, and skilled sailor, he loved a battle. His words, "I have not yet begun to fight," are famous throughout the world.

Jones was born on July 6, 1747, in Scotland. When only 12 years old, he was signed on as an apprentice aboard the *Friendship,* a merchant vessel sailing from England to the American colonies.

When the youth finished his apprenticeship, he joined the British navy. Then he became first mate on a slaver, a ship that carried slaves, but soon quit. Ashore in the West Indies, he became an actor. In a single season, he earned enough to sail home as a passenger. On the way, however, the captain and first mate died of typhoid fever. Jones was the only person aboard who could navigate a ship. He guided the ship into port, and the grateful owners kept him on as captain.

At port in the West Indies, Captain Jones had a sailor flogged for mutinous conduct. The sailor left the ship, took berth on another, and died some weeks later. Jones was blamed for the death. He fled his ship. In Virginia and North Carolina, he found old friends. Settling down, he led the placid life of a planter.

When the American Revolution started, he offered his services. His first command was the *Providence.* In 1777, he became captain of the sloop *Ranger.* He carried the news of British General John Bourgoyne's surrender to France. In France, he was given command of the converted merchant ship *Bonhomme Richard.*

On the afternoon of September 23, 1779, the *Bonhomme Richard* engaged the British 44-gun frigate *Serapis* in one of the most famous sea battles in history. For hours, the ships blazed away at each other at short range. Then Jones maneuvered to lash the bowsprit of the *Serapis* to his own ship. The *Bonhomme Richard* was badly damaged, and the English captain called upon Jones to surrender. Jones's proud reply has become a classic retort. "I have not yet begun to fight!" Victory came when an American sailor tossed an exploding grenade into a gunpowder magazine located just below the main deck of the *Serapis.*

After the war, Jones served the new American nation as its agent in Europe. His health was poor and he retired to Paris, where he died on July 18, 1792.

Reading Time _____

Recalling Facts

1. John Paul Jones is considered
   - ❏ a. the first Scottish sea captain.
   - ❏ b. the first great American naval hero.
   - ❏ c. a British sea captain during the Revolution.

2. Jones is famous for the words,
   - ❏ a. "If this be treason, make the most of it."
   - ❏ b. "But if they want war, then let it begin here."
   - ❏ c. "I have not yet begun to fight."

3. When only 12 years old, Jones apprenticed aboard a vessel sailing from
   - ❏ a. England to the American colonies.
   - ❏ b. the West Indies to Virginia.
   - ❏ c. the American colonies to France.

4. Jones's first command in the American Revolution was the ship
   - ❏ a. *Friendship*.
   - ❏ b. *Providence*.
   - ❏ c. *Ranger*.

5. The battle between the *Bonhomme Richard* and the *Serapis* was
   - ❏ a. a sea battle between France and Great Britain.
   - ❏ b. the last sea battle of the Revolutionary War.
   - ❏ c. one of the most famous sea battles in history.

Understanding Ideas

6. A word that describes John Paul Jones as a youth is
   - ❏ a. loyal.
   - ❏ b. studious.
   - ❏ c. adventurous.

7. Jones became a ship's captain due to
   - ❏ a. hard work.
   - ❏ b. luck.
   - ❏ c. wealth.

8. By offering his services to the American war effort, Jones showed his
   - ❏ a. cowardice.
   - ❏ b. patriotism.
   - ❏ c. stubbornness.

9. Jones's appointment as America's agent in Europe shows that he was
   - ❏ a. admired by his peers.
   - ❏ b. highly educated.
   - ❏ c. tired of fighting.

10. Jones's words during the battle with the *Serapis* suggest that he was
    - ❏ a. close to victory.
    - ❏ b. likely to surrender.
    - ❏ c. too proud to surrender.

The fourth child of a Scottish gardener, John Paul Jones always loved the sea. As a small boy, he hung around the local port, talking to sailors he met. According to one story, he arranged for his friends to fight a simulated naval battle in their rowboats as Jones stood on shore and shouted orders to them.

By the time he was twelve, Jones's formal education had ended. Without political connections or money, he could not go into the Royal Navy, but he could join the merchant marine. He agreed to work aboard a ship as an apprentice for seven years. He would receive little pay but would get an education in sailing. After three years, the ship was sold, and John Paul was released from his agreement.

John Paul's brother, a tailor, had moved to America. John Paul fell in love with the new country and decided that he would live there, too. He worked hard to lose his Scottish accent and studied to improve his writing style. He read widely. Meanwhile, he was improving his skills as a sailor, working on merchant ships that sailed to and from the West Indies. By the time he was 21 years old, Jones's experience and determination had made him an exceptional sailor.

1. **Recognizing Words in Context**

Find the word *simulated* in the passage. One definition below is a *synonym* for that word; it means the same or almost the same thing. One definition is an *antonym;* it has the opposite or nearly opposite meaning. The other has a completely different meaning. Label the definitions S for *synonym*, A for *antonym*, and D for *different*.

_____ a. together

_____ b. pretend

_____ c. real

2. **Distinguishing Fact from Opinion**

Two of the statements below present *facts,* which can be proved correct. The other statement is an *opinion,* which expresses someone's thoughts or beliefs. Label the statements F for *fact* and O for *opinion.*

_____ a. John Paul Jones joined the merchant marine.

_____ b. John Paul Jones agreed to work for seven years.

_____ c. John Paul Jones always loved the sea.

3. Keeping Events in Order

Label the statements below 1, 2, and 3 to show the order in which the events happened.

_____ a. John Paul Jones's formal education ended.

_____ b. John Paul Jones joined the merchant marine.

_____ c. John Paul Jones decided that he would live in America.

4. Making Correct Inferences

Two of the statements below are correct *inferences,* or reasonable guesses. They are based on information in the passage. The other statement is an incorrect, or faulty, inference. Label the statements C for *correct* inference and F for *faulty* inference.

_____ a. John Paul Jones set goals for himself.

_____ b. John Paul Jones worked hard at his job.

_____ c. John Paul Jones was unusually lucky.

5. Understanding Main Ideas

One of the statements below expresses the main idea of the passage. One statement is too general, or too broad. The other explains only part of the passage; it is too narrow. Label the statements M for *main idea,* B for *too broad,* and N for *too narrow.*

_____ a. John Paul Jones became a sailor at a young age.

_____ b. From an early age, John Paul Jones demonstrated a love of the sea and a willingness to learn that would make him successful.

_____ c. John Paul Jones worked to improve his speech and writing as well as his sailing skills.

Correct Answers, Part A _____

Correct Answers, Part B _____

Total Correct Answers _____

14   A   Swordfish

Found in tropical and temperate oceans around the world, the swordfish is large and powerful. It grows to about 15 feet (4.6 meters) in length and weighs between 150 and 1,000 pounds (68 to 454 kilograms). Occasionally specimens weighing more than 1,100 pounds (500 kilograms) have been reported.

The swordfish is named for its swordlike jaw extension. This bony, sharp-tipped extension of the upper jaw makes up about one-third of the fish's total length. Because the sword is flattened, rather than rounded as in the marlins and other spear-nosed fishes, it has given rise to a second common name for the swordfish: the broadbill.

The swordfish uses its sword to slash through a school of menhaden, herring, mackerel, or squid, killing or stunning its prey, which it then eats at leisure. The sword is also used to fight enemies.

Swordfish eggs are tiny floating globes about 1/16 of an inch (0.16 centimeter) in diameter. They hatch after about two and a half days. The baby swordfish bears little resemblance to the adult. Its body is covered with translucent scales and lined on either side with four rows of spiny plates. The dorsal fin runs the length of the body, and both jaws extend into slender swords of equal length. The baby has sharp teeth. By the time the fish is from 2 to 4 feet (0.6 to 1.2 meters) long, the scales, plates, and teeth disappear. An adult swordfish has no teeth at all. The single dorsal fin of the baby separates into a high, backward-curving lobe and a smaller fin on the tail. The lower jaw shortens and the upper jaw grows to a heavy, saberlike beak.

The color of both young and adult swordfish is gunmetal or bronze above and grayish or silvery below. The fins are dark and leathery. The sword is nearly black on top and paler underneath. Only the eyes of the swordfish are colorful. They are cobalt blue with a narrow rim of pale blue.

Swordfish generally live offshore, occasionally approaching close to the shore to feed. Although they are commonly considered solitary hunters, they sometimes travel or rest in pairs. These fish are often seen resting or swimming near the surface with their dorsal and upper caudal fins protruding above the water. They may descend to great depths, however, in search of food.

The swordfish is a prized food and big-game fish.

Reading Time _____

Recalling Facts

1. Swordfish are found
   - ❏ a. in tropical and temperate oceans.
   - ❏ b. in icy water.
   - ❏ c. only in the Atlantic Ocean.

2. Another name for a swordfish is the
   - ❏ a. herring.
   - ❏ b. broadbill.
   - ❏ c. mackerel.

3. The eyes of a swordfish are
   - ❏ a. silver.
   - ❏ b. black.
   - ❏ c. blue.

4. Swordfish generally live
   - ❏ a. close to shore.
   - ❏ b. offshore.
   - ❏ c. near islands.

5. The adult swordfish has
   - ❏ a. sharp teeth.
   - ❏ b. no teeth at all.
   - ❏ c. teeth of different sizes.

Understanding Ideas

6. Without its sword, the swordfish would find it hard to
   - ❏ a. swim.
   - ❏ b. feed.
   - ❏ c. mate.

7. It is likely that fishers enjoy catching swordfish because the fish
   - ❏ a. are easy to catch.
   - ❏ b. are very colorful.
   - ❏ c. put up a good fight.

8. To catch swordfish, a fishing boat should usually stay
   - ❏ a. close to shore.
   - ❏ b. offshore.
   - ❏ c. near islands.

9. The name *swordfish* suggests that
   - ❏ a. swordfish are the only fish with spearlike noses.
   - ❏ b. all fish have swordlike noses.
   - ❏ c. the upper jaw of a swordfish is a striking feature.

10. Swordfish may descend to great depths in search of food, which suggests that
    - ❏ a. food may be scarce.
    - ❏ b. swordfish like deep water.
    - ❏ c. swordfish are solitary hunters.

The young swordfish swam silently in search of food. Just ahead, the fish
sensed the presence of a school of herring. It increased its speed as hunger
drove it on. The swordfish had not yet reached its full length of 15 feet
(4.6 m), but it was still almost the length of two people. Now it needed
food to fuel its silvery body.

As the swordfish dove into the mass of herring, it became aware of other
huge, dark shapes descending on the school. The panicked herring had
attracted the attention of other predators. Stopping its own attack on the
herring, the swordfish whirled to face the tooth-filled jaws of a blue shark!
The shark, one of the fiercest predators in the sea, was as large as the
swordfish. The swordfish's only hope was to get in the first blow. With a
surge of its powerful muscles, the swordfish thrust its sword, raking it along
the shark's side. Blood clouded the water.

The swordfish dove deep, away from the wounded shark. The other
sharks, attracted by the scent of blood, swarmed around it. The predator
had become prey to its own kind. The swordfish swam away to find a meal
of its own.

1. **Recognizing Words in Context**

    Find the word *kind* in the passage.
    One definition below is a *synonym* for
    that word; it means the same or
    almost the same thing. One definition
    is an *antonym;* it has the opposite or
    nearly opposite meaning. The other
    has a completely different meaning.
    Label the definitions S for *synonym,*
    A for *antonym,* and D for *different.*

    _____ a. strangers

    _____ b. friendly

    _____ c. group

2. **Distinguishing Fact from Opinion**

    Two of the statements below present
    facts, which can be proved correct.
    The other statement is an *opinion,*
    which expresses someone's thoughts
    or beliefs. Label the statements F for
    fact and O for *opinion.*

    _____ a. A swordfish is a nicer fish
    than a shark.

    _____ b. The swordfish was almost
    the length of two people.

    _____ c. A blue shark is one of the
    fiercest predators in the sea.

3. Keeping Events in Order

Two of the statements below describe events that happened at the same time. The other statement describes an event that happened before or after those events. Label them S for *same time,* B for *before,* and A for *after.*

_____ a. The swordfish dove toward the school of herring.

_____ b. The swordfish whirled to face the jaws of a shark.

_____ c. Sharks descended toward the herring.

4. Making Correct Inferences

Two of the statements below are correct *inferences,* or reasonable guesses. They are based on information in the passage. The other statement is an incorrect, or faulty, inference. Label the statements C for *correct* inference and F for *faulty* inference.

_____ a. A swordfish can use its sword to protect itself from enemies.

_____ b. Sharks will attack and eat their own kind if they are wounded.

_____ c. In a battle between a shark and a swordfish, the swordfish will always win.

5. Understanding Main Ideas

One of the statements below expresses the main idea of the passage. One statement is too general, or too broad. The other explains only part of the passage; it is too narrow. Label the statements M for *main idea,* B for *too broad,* and N for *too narrow.*

_____ a. A swordfish, under attack from a shark, saved itself with its sword.

_____ b. The swordfish thrust its sword, raking it along the shark's side.

_____ c. Sharks and swordfish prey on other fish.

Correct Answers, Part A _____

Correct Answers, Part B _____

Total Correct Answers _____

Ships of the Desert

For thousands of years, the camel has helped people live in the deserts of Asia and Africa. It can travel great distances over hot sands for days without water. It can carry a person or a load of freight. For this reason, it is sometimes called the "ship of the desert."

The camel supplies food and many valuable materials to desert dwellers. These people can live for many weeks on thick, cheesy camel's milk and on the meat of young camels. Desert dwellers make camel's hair into tents, blankets, rugs, clothing, and rope and cord. Dried camel droppings supply fuel for cooking fires. When a camel dies, its hide is used for making sandals, water bags, and many other necessities.

There are two kinds of camels. The dromedary, or Arabian, camel has a single hump on its back. The Asian camel has two humps. The dromedary once roamed wild but is now found only in domestication. Groups of them, however, are often left on their own for up to five months. The Asian camel is primarily a domesticated animal, but small wild herds are still found in areas of Mongolia and China. Only about 300 to 500 Asian camels still live in a wild state, so the species is considered in danger of extinction.

Although often ill tempered, the camel is wonderfully adapted for the work it has to do. No other animal can live and work on such scant supplies of food and water in so hot and dry a climate.

One of the few things that a camel will do on command is kneel. It is easier for a person to climb onto or load up the animal when it kneels. The camel seldom works without a protest. The uproar in a camel yard when a caravan is being loaded is deafening.

The camel's most striking feature is the large hump or humps on its back. The hump is formed of fat and muscle. When a camel is well fed and given enough water, the hump is erect. If the camel has to go without food and water for a period of time, the hump becomes limp and leans to one side.

The camel's body is covered with a shaggy, sand-colored coat. The hair sheds in great handfuls, giving the animal a perpetually frowsy look. Long eyelashes protect the eyes from sandstorms and the glare of the desert sun.

Reading Time _____

Recalling Facts

1. Items such as tents, rugs, and rope are made from camel
   - ❏ a. hair.
   - ❏ b. hides.
   - ❏ c. droppings.

2. A two-humped camel is called
   - ❏ a. an Asian camel.
   - ❏ b. a dromedary.
   - ❏ c. an Arabian camel.

3. Camels are known for their
   - ❏ a. obedience.
   - ❏ b. good nature.
   - ❏ c. ill temper.

4. On command, a camel will
   - ❏ a. run.
   - ❏ b. kneel.
   - ❏ c. work.

5. Today most camels are
   - ❏ a. found in the wild.
   - ❏ b. domesticated.
   - ❏ c. found in zoos.

Understanding Ideas

6. Camels are called "ships of the desert" because of their
   - ❏ a. resemblance to large ships.
   - ❏ b. ability to go without water.
   - ❏ c. usefulness as transportation.

7. The number of Asian camels is
   - ❏ a. greater than the number of Arabian camels.
   - ❏ b. about the same as the number of Arabian camels.
   - ❏ c. less than the number of Arabian camels.

8. You can conclude from the article that a camel's hump
   - ❏ a. serves no special function.
   - ❏ b. stores food and water.
   - ❏ c. makes it ill tempered.

9. It is likely that in a nondesert climate, the camel would be regarded as
   - ❏ a. a popular means of transportation.
   - ❏ b. an unpopular means of transportation.
   - ❏ c. an ideal substitute for a horse.

10. You can conclude that a camel's height is usually
    - ❏ a. greater than a human's.
    - ❏ b. less than a human's.
    - ❏ c. about the same as a human's.

Camels in America

In the mid-1800s, Major Henry C. Wayne had what he thought was a terrific idea. Wayne had read about camels and their ability to survive in desert areas. He thought camels would be perfect for carrying goods across the hot, dry southwestern United States. Wayne managed to convince his superiors that his idea was worth trying. U.S. Secretary of War Jefferson Davis agreed. In 1856, 34 camels arrived in Texas. They were followed by another 41 animals a year later.

Wayne was right. The camels performed perfectly. They carried heavier loads than horses and mules. They happily ate cacti and other plant life that no horse or mule would touch. On long journeys, they arrived in better health than the other animals. They were a great success.

There was just one problem. Everyone hated the camels. The animals were stubborn, smelly, and noisy. When loaded and unloaded, the camels let out loud groans. Army horses refused to stay in the same stables with camels. When the Civil War broke out four years after camels were introduced, the experiment came to an end. After the war, railroads replaced animal caravans. Some people claim, however, that wild camels descended from the Army veterans are still roaming the Southwest.

1. Recognizing Words in Context

Find the word *trying* in the passage. One definition below is a *synonym* for that word; it means the same or almost the same thing. One definition is an *antonym;* it has the opposite or nearly opposite meaning. The other has a completely different meaning. Label the definitions S for *synonym*, A for *antonym*, and D for *different*.

_____ a. avoiding

_____ b. attempting

_____ c. bothersome

2. Distinguishing Fact from Opinion

Two of the statements below present *facts*, which can be proved correct. The other statement is an *opinion,* which expresses someone's thoughts or beliefs. Label the statements F for *fact* and O for *opinion*.

_____ a. Camels carried heavier loads than horses and mules.

_____ b. Camels are stubborn, smelly, and noisy.

_____ c. Everyone hated the camels.

3. Keeping Events in Order

Label the statements below 1, 2, and 3 to show the order in which the events happened.

_____ a. Thirty-four camels arrived in Texas.

_____ b. The Civil War started.

_____ c. Major Wayne thought camels could be used to carry goods in the Southwest.

4. Making Correct Inferences

Two of the statements below are correct *inferences,* or reasonable guesses. They are based on information in the passage. The other statement is an incorrect, or faulty, inference. Label the statements C for *correct* inference and F for *faulty* inference.

_____ a. Camels are well suited to living in the southwestern United States.

_____ b. In desert areas, camels make better pack animals than do horses and mules.

_____ c. If you visit the Southwest, you can see wild camels.

5. Understanding Main Ideas

One of the statements below expresses the main idea of the passage. One statement is too general, or too broad. The other explains only part of the passage; it is too narrow. Label the statements M for *main idea,* B for *too broad,* and N for *too narrow.*

_____ a. Camels are perfectly adapted for life in the desert.

_____ b. The camels ate cacti and other desert plants that horses and mules would not eat.

_____ c. The U.S. Army experimented with camels as draft animals before the Civil War; but although the animals performed well, no one liked them.

Correct Answers, Part A _____

Correct Answers, Part B _____

Total Correct Answers _____

For many centuries, the sword was the chief weapon of war. Defenses against it were gradually invented. The best defense was another sword. Next, a stout shield was found to be a great help. Early shields were made of heavy leather over a wood framework. Later came metal shields. A defender used the shield to parry the blow of an opponent's sword while driving home his own weapon. The shield eventually grew larger and longer. A warrior could hide almost completely behind it. But this type of shield proved too heavy and unwieldy. With it, a battler could move only slowly and with great difficulty.

To use a three-foot (1-meter) sword effectively, a fighter had to be within three feet of the enemy. At such short distances, however, the fighter was in turn easily within reach of the opponent's sword. Being able to fight at greater distances would protect the fighters. They gained this distance by using spears, javelins, lances, and similar weapons with sharp points on long shafts. Spears were lightweight and well balanced so that they could be thrown with great accuracy.

Longer and heavier spears were used for thrusting rather than throwing. They were especially deadly when held firmly in the grip of a horse rider moving at full tilt. With the horse, warriors gained the advantage of speed and movement in battle.

During the Middle Ages, armed and armored knights on horseback became the heroic figures of warfare. The spears they used were so long and heavy that the knights rested them on saddle braces. At this time, playing at war became more popular than war itself. Great jousting tournaments were held at the principal courts of Europe. At these celebrated events, special jousting spears were used. They were blunt-ended, and the opponents were well covered with armor so that little blood was spilled.

Suits of armor were cleverly made so that overlapping steel plates allowed bending of joints and easier movement than one might suspect. Even horses were armored. A knight in heavy armor was at great risk, however, when thrown from a horse. On the ground, the knight could easily be surrounded by serfs armed with pikes. Pikes were spears up to twenty-four feet (7 meters) in length. They were carried by the lowly infantry, which made up most of the fighting force. Only the rich and lordly rode out to battle in shining armor.

Reading Time _____

Recalling Facts

1. The best defense against a sword was
   - ❏ a. another sword.
   - ❏ b. a spear.
   - ❏ c. a stout shield.

2. The earliest shields were made of
   - ❏ a. strong cloth on wood.
   - ❏ b. metal.
   - ❏ c. heavy leather.

3. Spears used for thrusting rather than throwing were
   - ❏ a. shorter and heavier.
   - ❏ b. shorter and lighter.
   - ❏ c. longer and heavier.

4. During the Middle Ages, the heroic figures in warfare were the
   - ❏ a. knights.
   - ❏ b. infantry soldiers.
   - ❏ c. serfs.

5. The infantry was composed of
   - ❏ a. knights.
   - ❏ b. lords.
   - ❏ c. serfs.

Understanding Ideas

6. You can conclude from the article that the best weapon for close combat was a
   - ❏ a. jousting spear.
   - ❏ b. sword.
   - ❏ c. javelin.

7. A soldier in armor and on horseback was probably
   - ❏ a. from the lower classes.
   - ❏ b. a member of the upper classes.
   - ❏ c. in the infantry.

8. You can conclude that armor and a shield
   - ❏ a. prevented bloodshed.
   - ❏ b. were useful only for horseback riders.
   - ❏ c. helped prevent bloodshed.

9. You can conclude that very large metal shields
   - ❏ a. had both advantages and disadvantages.
   - ❏ b. were more troublesome than helpful.
   - ❏ c. were best suited for poor fighters.

10. The article suggests that during the Middle Ages, war was considered
   - ❏ a. shameful.
   - ❏ b. amusing.
   - ❏ c. extravagant.

A fifteenth-century knight who wanted a suit of armor visited an armorer. The armorer kept metal forms for arms, legs, heads, and bodies of different sizes. After measuring a knight, the armorer chose the forms that would fit best. Then a suit of armor was built around these.

The armorer began by hammering steel bars called billets into thin sheets. Then these sheets were cut to size. Next, they were heated and hammered into shape over the metal forms the armorer had chosen.

The main pieces then went to joiners. Joiners cut smaller metal pieces and connected them to the main pieces with rivets. They were joined in a way that would allow a knight to move his arms and legs. The joiners created a delicate series of movable plates to cover the knight's feet and hands—even separate armor for the thumb. They designed pieces to protect the neck and head that also allowed the wearer to see and breathe easily. Finally, finishers polished the armor, put in padding for comfort, and added decorations.

A complete suit of armor might have more than 200 separate pieces. Looking at armor today, you may wonder how a knight could move at all! However, battle armor was reasonably comfortable and light—about 45 to 60 pounds (20 to 27 kg). This is about the same amount of weight as a modern soldier's gear has.

1. **Recognizing Words in Context**

   Find the word *light* in the passage. One definition below is a *synonym* for that word; it means the same or almost the same thing. One definition is an *antonym;* it has the opposite or nearly opposite meaning. The other has a completely different meaning. Label the definitions S for *synonym,* A for *antonym,* and D for *different.*

   _____ a. heavy

   _____ b. amusing

   _____ c. weighing little

2. **Distinguishing Fact from Opinion**

   Two of the statements below present *facts,* which can be proved correct. The other statement is an *opinion,* which expresses someone's thoughts or beliefs. Label the statements F for *fact* and O for *opinion.*

   _____ a. The armorer hammered steel bars into thin sheets.

   _____ b. It seems impossible that a knight in armor could move at all.

   _____ c. A complete suit of armor might have more than 200 separate pieces.

3. **Keeping Events in Order**

Label the statements below 1, 2, and 3 to show the order in which the events happened.

_____ a. The suit of armor was padded and decorated.

_____ b. The armorer hammered bars of steel into thin sheets.

_____ c. Joiners created movable joints for the suit's arms and legs.

4. **Making Correct Inferences**

Two of the statements below are correct *inferences,* or reasonable guesses. They are based on information in the passage. The other statement is an incorrect, or faulty, inference. Label the statements C for *correct* inference and F for *faulty* inference.

_____ a. Everyone in the fifteenth century wore armor.

_____ b. A suit of armor protected the knight's whole body.

_____ c. Making a suit of armor was a highly skilled craft.

5. **Understanding Main Ideas**

One of the statements below expresses the main idea of the passage. One statement is too general, or too broad. The other explains only part of the passage; it is too narrow. Label the statements M for *main idea,* B for *too broad,* and N for *too narrow.*

_____ a. Making a suit of armor worn by a fifteenth-century knight required the labor of armorers, joiners, and finishers.

_____ b. By the beginning of the fifteenth century, knights wore full suits of plate armor into battle.

_____ c. Large pieces of armor were put together by joiners, who connected them with smaller metal pieces to create movable joints.

Correct Answers, Part A _____

Correct Answers, Part B _____

Total Correct Answers _____

Try Jogging for Fitness

Running for fitness, exercise, and pleasure is commonly called jogging. It has become very popular in recent years. The popularity of jogging today stems from several factors. First, jogging is one of the most efficient forms of exercise. As a rule, a person jogging burns up more calories per minute than in most other sports. Running, like biking, swimming, and brisk walking, is an aerobic exercise. Such an exercise uses a great deal of oxygen. In addition, it increases the heart rate. Aerobic exercise strengthens the heart muscle so that it pumps more efficiently. This kind of exercise is also one of the best ways to improve the general health and capacity of the lungs.

Jogging is also popular because almost everyone can take part. Jogging is an activity that doesn't require any unusual skills or special coordination. Jogging is relaxing and fun. Finally, it can be done alone, with another person, or in a group.

The same number of calories (about 100 for most men and 80 for most women) is burned walking a mile as running a mile. Thus, one of the best ways to begin a jogging program is to combine it with a walking program. Increases in the amount of jogging should come gradually. The jogger who experiences dizziness, tightness of the chest, or nausea should slow down. If the discomfort is great, the jogger should consult a doctor before running again.

For anyone who runs more than 10 miles (16 kilometers) a week, it is important to have good running shoes. Tennis shoes or sneakers won't do. Running produces stress that is 3 times greater than the stress of walking. With this added stress to the feet and legs, a jogger needs good shoes. The shoes should be replaced when they are worn out or worn unevenly.

Cold weather poses few problems for joggers. The main hazard in winter running is slipping on ice or snow. There is no danger of freezing the lungs, because the body warms the air before it reaches the lungs. Winter joggers should be sure to cover the head and extremities and keep their feet as dry and warm as possible. It is best to wear layers of clothing.

In summer, joggers must be careful not to dry out. Drinking plenty of water on hot, humid days is important. The best summer wear is loose fitting and light colored.

Reading Time _____

Recalling Facts

1. Aerobic exercise increases
   - ❏ a. the size of the heart.
   - ❏ b. the heart rate.
   - ❏ c. chest tightness.

2. Briskly walking a mile burns about
   - ❏ a. 8 to 10 calories.
   - ❏ b. 80 to 100 calories.
   - ❏ c. 800 to 1,000 calories.

3. Jogging is a popular form of exercise in part because it
   - ❏ a. takes very little time.
   - ❏ b. is an inefficient form of exercise.
   - ❏ c. requires no special skills.

4. The stress of running is
   - ❏ a. three times greater than the stress of walking.
   - ❏ b. three times less than the stress of walking.
   - ❏ c. about the same as the stress of walking.

5. The main hazard of winter running is
   - ❏ a. freezing the lungs.
   - ❏ b. cold, wet feet.
   - ❏ c. slipping on ice or snow.

Understanding Ideas

6. One of the best ways to stay in shape is by
   - ❏ a. burning up calories.
   - ❏ b. exercising aerobically.
   - ❏ c. working out for long periods of time.

7. It is likely that people like jogging because
   - ❏ a. it causes heavy breathing.
   - ❏ b. doctors recommend it.
   - ❏ c. it is an easy way to stay in shape.

8. To get the most from the exercise, joggers should
   - ❏ a. increase their heart rate.
   - ❏ b. train for several weeks.
   - ❏ c. run as fast as they can.

9. Good running shoes are important because
   - ❏ a. joggers can run faster.
   - ❏ b. they keep the feet warm and dry.
   - ❏ c. they help absorb the stress of jogging.

10. You can conclude from the article that jogging is popular
    - ❏ a. mostly in warm-weather areas.
    - ❏ b. in a variety of climates.
    - ❏ c. mostly in cold-weather areas.

At the age of 72, Noel Johnson was 40 pounds overweight. He smoked cigarettes and had a heart condition. He was in such bad shape that his doctor gave him six months to live. Johnson's son wanted him to go into a retirement home. "That's not necessary!" Johnson said. "I'm fine."

"Well, will you show me you can walk?" his son responded.

Johnson started walking every day. Each day he walked a little farther and a little faster. Within a few months he was running three or four miles a day. When his doctor tested him again, his heart was beating at a healthy 63 beats a minute.

The fitness bug had bitten Johnson. In addition to running, he began working out on an exercise bike and a treadmill. At the age of 80, he ran in the New York City marathon and became the first 80-year-old to complete the 26-mile run. Now 92, Johnson has run in eight marathons, written several books, and lectured in countries all around the world. One of his goals is to run a marathon when he reaches the age of 100. "I know I'll be in better condition then than I am now," he says.

1. **Recognizing Words in Context**

   Find the word *beating* in the passage. One definition below is a *synonym* for that word; it means the same or almost the same thing. One definition is an *antonym;* it has the opposite or nearly opposite meaning. The other has a completely different meaning. Label the definitions S for *synonym*, A for *antonym,* and D for *different*.

   _____ a. stopped

   _____ b. thrashing

   _____ c. pulsing

2. **Distinguishing Fact from Opinion**

   Two of the statements below present *facts*, which can be proved correct. The other statement is an *opinion*, which expresses someone's thoughts or beliefs. Label the statements F for *fact* and O for *opinion*.

   _____ a. Noel Johnson was the first 80-year-old to finish a 26-mile marathon.

   _____ b. Noel Johnson is an example that it is never too late to make changes in your life-style.

   _____ c. At the age of 72, Noel Johnson was overweight and in poor health.

3. **Keeping Events in Order**

Label the statements below 1, 2, and 3 to show the order in which the events happened.

_____ a. Johnson began walking every day.

_____ b. Johnson ran in the New York City marathon.

_____ c. Johnson ran three or four miles a day.

4. **Making Correct Inferences**

Two of the statements below are correct *inferences,* or reasonable guesses. They are based on information in the passage. The other statement is an incorrect, or faulty, inference. Label the statements C for *correct* inference and F for *faulty* inference.

_____ a. Any 80-year-old who takes up jogging can complete a marathon.

_____ b. Johnson's fitness plan paid off in improved health.

_____ c. Old age does not have to mean illness and lack of physical fitness.

5. **Understanding Main Ideas**

One of the statements below expresses the main idea of the passage. One statement is too general, or too broad. The other explains only part of the passage; it is too narrow. Label the statements M for *main idea,* B for *too broad,* and N for *too narrow.*

_____ a. Noel Johnson changed his life-style at the age of 72 and became physically fit enough to run marathons.

_____ b. Jogging is one of the most efficient forms of exercise.

_____ c. Noel Johnson began walking every day to prove that he did not belong in a retirement home.

Correct Answers, Part A _____

Correct Answers, Part B _____

Total Correct Answers _____

Achilles

Among the Greeks who fought against Troy, the one considered the bravest was Achilles. His mother was the goddess Thetis. His father was Peleus, king of Thessaly. The king was a grandson of Zeus, the lord of Heaven.

Soon after the birth of Achilles, Thetis tried to outwit the Fates, who had foretold that war would cut down her son in his prime. So that no weapon might ever wound him, she dipped her baby in the black waters of the Styx. This was the river that flowed around the underworld. Only the heel by which she held him was untouched by the magic waters. This was the only part of his body that could be wounded. This is the source of the expressions *Achilles' heel,* meaning "a vulnerable point."

When the Trojan War began, Achilles' mother, fearing that the decree of the Fates would prove true, dressed Achilles as a girl. She hid him among the maidens at the court of the king. The trick did not succeed. Odysseus, the shrewdest of the Greeks, went to the court disguised as a peddler. When he had spread his wares before the girls, a sudden trumpet blast was sounded. The girls screamed and fled, but Achilles betrayed his sex by seizing a sword and spear from the peddler's stock.

Achilles joined the battle and took command of the Myrmidons. They set an example of bravery for the other Greeks. Then he quarreled with Agamemnon, the leader of the Greeks, over a captive whom Achilles loved. When she was taken from him, Achilles withdrew his followers from the fight and sulked in his tent. As a result, the Greek armies were driven back to their ships by the Trojans.

At last, moved by the plight of the Greeks, Achilles entrusted his forces and his armor to Patroclus, his best friend. When Patroclus led the Myrmidons into battle, the Trojans mistook him for Achilles and fled in panic. However, they were able to continue fighting with the help of other nations. Achilles broke the strength of these allies by killing Memnon, prince of the Ethiopians, and Penthesilea, queen of the Amazons.

Achilles was now weary of war and moreover, had fallen in love with Polyxena. He was in the temple arranging for his marriage when an enemy shot him with a poisoned arrow in the only vulnerable part of his body— the heel.

Reading Time _____

Recalling Facts

1. Achilles' father was
   - ❏ a. king of Thessaly.
   - ❏ b. a Trojan.
   - ❏ c. a son of Zeus.

2. The expression *Achilles' heel* means
   - ❏ a. a dangerous weapon.
   - ❏ b. a kind of armor.
   - ❏ c. a vulnerable point.

3. Agamemnon was
   - ❏ a. a Greek military leader.
   - ❏ b. ruler of Troy.
   - ❏ c. Achilles' best friend.

4. To protect her son, Achilles' mother
   - ❏ a. disguised him as a peddler.
   - ❏ b. hid him among the maidens at the court of the king.
   - ❏ c. sent him to Troy.

5. Achilles died as the result of
   - ❏ a. a poisoned arrow.
   - ❏ b. an infection in his foot.
   - ❏ c. old age.

Understanding Ideas

6. Thetis dipped Achilles in the black waters of the Styx, which shows that
   - ❏ a. the Styx was polluted.
   - ❏ b. Thetis was superstitious.
   - ❏ c. Thetis was a practical woman.

7. Achilles can best be described as
   - ❏ a. a brave warrior with human flaws.
   - ❏ b. a cowardly person.
   - ❏ c. pompous and overbearing.

8. The story of Achilles should be considered
   - ❏ a. a Greek legend.
   - ❏ b. a true story.
   - ❏ c. historically correct.

9. You can conclude from the article that in ancient Greece arguments were often settled
   - ❏ a. in court.
   - ❏ b. on the battlefield.
   - ❏ c. by negotiation.

10. The story of Achilles suggests that the Greeks believed that
    - ❏ a. people's lives are controlled by fate.
    - ❏ b. love conquers all.
    - ❏ c. gods and goddesses are all-powerful.

As a child in Germany, Heinrich Schliemann read a book about the fall of Troy. It had pictures of the burning city. "There must be something left," he said.

"It's just a story," his father told him.

"When I grow up, I'm going to find Troy," Heinrich announced.

Heinrich Schliemann became a successful businessperson. But he never forgot about Troy. In 1863, when he was 46 years old, he sold his business. Eventually, he moved to Greece and learned to speak Greek. Then he went to find Troy.

Schliemann used a poem by Homer about the war in Troy to help him find the city. His search finally led him to a small hill called Hissarlik in Asia Minor.

Schliemann hired over a hundred workers to excavate the hill. What they found amazed everyone. Within the hill were the ruins of nine cities that over time had been built one on top of the other. The ruins of one city contained gold, silver, and jewels. That city had been destroyed by fire. A triumphant Schliemann announced that he had found the city of Troy.

Later, scholars decided that the real Troy was on another level. But Schliemann had proved that Troy was more than just a story.

1. **Recognizing Words in Context**

    Find the word *excavate* in the passage. One definition below is a *synonym* for that word; it means the same or almost the same thing. One definition is an *antonym;* it has the opposite or nearly opposite meaning. The other has a completely different meaning. Label the definitions S for *synonym*, A for *antonym*, and D for *different.*

    _____ a. bury

    _____ b. unearth

    _____ c. examine

2. **Distinguishing Fact from Opinion**

    Two of the statements below present *facts*, which can be proved correct. The other statement is an *opinion*, which expresses someone's thoughts or beliefs. Label the statements F for *fact* and O for *opinion*.

    _____ a. Schliemann dug at Hissarlik.

    _____ b. Schliemann's workers uncovered nine cities.

    _____ c. What the workers found amazed everyone.

3. Keeping Events in Order

Label the statements below 1, 2, and 3 to show the order in which the events happened.

_____ a. Schliemann's workers uncovered ancient cities.

_____ b. Schliemann became a successful businessperson.

_____ c. Schliemann announced that he found Troy.

4. Making Correct Inferences

Two of the statements below are correct *inferences,* or reasonable guesses. They are based on information in the passage. The other statement is an incorrect, or faulty, inference. Label the statements C for *correct* inference and F for *faulty* inference.

_____ a. Schliemann was a very determined person.

_____ b. Schliemann found the same city he had read about as a boy.

_____ c. Schliemann was right to think that something of Troy had been left behind.

5. Understanding Main Ideas

One of the statements below expresses the main idea of the passage. One statement is too general, or too broad. The other explains only part of the passage; it is too narrow. Label the statements M for *main idea,* B for *too broad,* and N for *too narrow.*

_____ a. Heinrich Schliemann used a poem by Homer to help him find Troy.

_____ b. Some stories are based on truth.

_____ c. Because Heinrich Schliemann never stopped believing in its existence, he found the place where Troy may have been.

Correct Answers, Part A _____

Correct Answers, Part B _____

Total Correct Answers _____

Transportation is something that touches everyone's life. Machines play an ever-increasing role in it. Trucks carry goods along the highways. Jets streak across the United States in about four hours. Great liners plow the seas at impressive speeds. Diesel trains roar over the rails from the Atlantic to the Pacific.

Today most people take transportation machines for granted. But it was not so long ago that people didn't have these machines. At first, everyone walked and carried loads on his or her back. Then people began to train animals. Soon travelers could ride horses, camels, or donkeys. Pack animals carried their baggage.

After the invention of the wheel, people built carts and wagons. With these wheeled vehicles, much larger loads could be carried. Still, for hundreds of years, land transportation was limited by the speed and strength of some draft animal.

Meanwhile, seafarers had known for centuries how to harness the wind. As time passed, shipwrights learned how to build bigger and faster sailing ships. Even so, when there was no wind, the nineteenth-century clipper ship captain was no better off than the ancient Egyptian on a Nile barge.

Then, in 1829, George Stephenson from England thought of mounting one of the new steam engines on a set of wheels. His little locomotive was able to pull a train of small cars along a track at about twenty miles (thirty-two kilometers) an hour. This was faster than anyone had ever traveled over land before. The railroad age had dawned.

At about the same time, American inventor Robert Fulton mounted a steam engine in a boat. The engine turned a pair of paddle wheels. Steamboats were soon puffing up and down all of the great rivers. They carried passengers and freight from town to town.

Steamboats were used on the seas, too. Paddle-wheel ocean steamers always carried masts and sails in case they ran out of wood. Later, screw-propeller vessels, which burned coal, were used.

The steam engine became so improved that it seemed it would forever remain the chief means of powering transportation machines. But then the gasoline engine was invented. Instead of getting power from expanding steam, this engine worked by explosions of gasoline vapor. The gas engine opened the door for the modern automobile, truck, and airplane. Yet, the gas engine would soon meet stiff competition from the diesel engine. Together they would power most means of modern transportation.

Reading Time _____

Recalling Facts

1. The first sources of transportation were
   - ❑ a. boats.
   - ❑ b. animals.
   - ❑ c. carts.

2. The invention of the wheel made it possible to
   - ❑ a. move larger loads.
   - ❑ b. eliminate pack animals.
   - ❑ c. harness the wind.

3. Nineteenth-century clipper ships depended on
   - ❑ a. steam power.
   - ❑ b. wind power.
   - ❑ c. gas power.

4. George Stephenson invented a
   - ❑ a. steamboat.
   - ❑ b. steam locomotive.
   - ❑ c. gas engine.

5. A fuel not used by ocean steamers was
   - ❑ a. wood.
   - ❑ b. coal.
   - ❑ c. gas.

Understanding Ideas

6. You can conclude from the article that the biggest influence on transportation has been
   - ❑ a. animals.
   - ❑ b. machines.
   - ❑ c. the steam engine.

7. From the article, you can conclude that wind power is
   - ❑ a. an efficient source of power.
   - ❑ b. an unreliable source of power.
   - ❑ c. no longer used as a source of power.

8. A secondary power source for paddle-wheel ocean steamers was
   - ❑ a. water.
   - ❑ b. gas.
   - ❑ c. wind.

9. The article suggests that transportation is
   - ❑ a. necessary to the modern way of life.
   - ❑ b. a necessary evil.
   - ❑ c. more a luxury than a necessity.

10. It is likely that the transportation industry
    - ❑ a. will benefit from new inventions.
    - ❑ b. has reached its limits.
    - ❑ c. will emphasize the past rather than the future.

Moving with Machines

More than a hundred years ago, two engineers came up with the same idea. They decided to put an engine on a vehicle. The engineers were Karl Benz and Gottlieb Daimler. Both lived in Germany, but they worked independently of one another. They developed some of the world's first motor-powered vehicles. Within forty years of their work, horse-drawn carriages were becoming a thing of the past. They were gradually being replaced with automobiles.

In 1885, Daimler attached a half-horsepower engine to a wooden bicycle. Although the ride was bumpy, this early motorcycle moved under its own power. In 1886, Daimler made what became known as a "horseless carriage." He equipped a horse carriage with an engine. Carrying four adults, the Daimler car could travel about 10 miles an hour (16 kilometers per hour). Daimler formed an auto manufacturing company in 1890. In 1901, he introduced the Mercedes automobile.

Meanwhile in 1878, Benz had begun his auto-making career by mounting a gasoline engine on a large tricycle. Benz successfully demonstrated his vehicle on the streets of Mannheim, Germany, in 1885. Later he improved on this design and built a four-wheeled vehicle. By 1891, people were buying factory-built Benz motorcars.

In 1926, Daimler and Benz joined forces. They merged their companies to form Daimler-Benz & Company.

1. Recognizing Words in Context

Find the word *power* in the passage. One definition below is a *synonym* for that word; it means the same or almost the same thing. One definition is an *antonym;* it has the opposite or nearly opposite meaning. The other has a completely different meaning. Label the definitions S for *synonym*, A for *antonym,* and D for *different*.

_____ a. ability

_____ b. powerlessness

_____ c. strength

2. Distinguishing Fact from Opinion

Two of the statements below present *facts,* which can be proved correct. The other statement is an *opinion,* which expresses someone's thoughts or beliefs. Label the statements F for *fact* and O for *opinion*.

_____ a. Trying to make a carriage that ran by itself was a silly idea.

_____ b. Karl Benz mounted a gasoline engine on a tricycle.

_____ c. Daimler attached an engine to a wooden bicycle frame.

3. Keeping Events in Order

Two of the statements below describe events that happened at the same time. The other statement describes an event that happened before or after those events. Label them S for *same time,* B for *before,* and A for *after.*

_____ a. Daimler invented a motorcycle by attaching an engine to a bicycle.

_____ b. People bought factory-built Benz automobiles.

_____ c. Benz demonstrated his motor-driven tricycle by driving it through Mannheim.

4. Making Correct Inferences

Two of the statements below are correct *inferences,* or reasonable guesses. They are based on information in the passage. The other statement is an incorrect, or faulty, inference. Label the statements C for *correct* inference and F for *faulty* inference.

_____ a. Inventors sometimes come up with the same idea working independently of each other.

_____ b. It took a while for people to become used to the idea of motor-powered vehicles.

_____ c. After automobiles were invented, people never used horses to pull carriages.

5. Understanding Main Ideas

One of the statements below expresses the main idea of the passage. One statement is too general, or too broad. The other explains only part of the passage; it is too narrow. Label the statements M for *main idea,* B for *too broad,* and N for *too narrow.*

_____ a. Daimler's first car could travel about 10 miles an hour (16 km/hour).

_____ b. The development of the modern automobile was shaped over many years by advances in engineering.

_____ c. Working independently of each other, the German engineers Karl Benz and Gottlieb Daimler invented and developed some of the world's first motor-powered vehicles.

Correct Answers, Part A _____

Correct Answers, Part B _____

Total Correct Answers _____

The Mighty Plant

Wherever there is sunlight, air, and soil, plants can be found. On the northernmost coast of Greenland, the Arctic poppy peeps out from beneath the ice. Mosses and tussock grasses grow in Antarctica. Flowers of vivid colors and great variety force their way up through the snow on mountainsides. Many shrubs and cacti thrive in deserts that go without rain for years at a time. Rivers, lakes, and swamps are filled with water plants. There are few places on the earth where plants have not been known to grow.

Botanists, the scientists who study plants, have named and described nearly 500,000 different kinds of plants. They estimate that another 500,000 undiscovered species exist in less explored ecosystems such as tropical forests. In addition, about 2,000 new plants are discovered or developed every year.

Human beings are completely dependent upon plants. Directly or indirectly, plants provide the food, clothing, fuel, shelter, and other necessities of life. People's direct dependence on crops such as wheat and corn is obvious. These crops are used to make many food products including breads and pastas. But without grass and grain, the livestock that provide people with food and other animal products could not survive either.

The food that plants store for their own growth is also the food that humans and other organisms need. In North America, the chief food plants are cereal grains such as corn, wheat, oats, rice, barley, rye, and buckwheat. Legumes are the second greatest source of food from plants. Legumes such as peas, beans, soybeans, and peanuts are high in protein and oil. Sago, taro, and cassava are major starchy foods for people in certain tropical places. Seaweeds are an important part of the diet in some cultures, especially in Asia.

Most seasonings are derived from plant materials. People have used herbs and spices for centuries to flavor and preserve food. Some seasonings, such as pepper and nutmeg, are obtained from dried fruits. Others, including thyme, sage, and rosemary, come from leaves. Plant stems provide such spices as ginger and cinnamon.

Most beverages also come from plants. Coffee and tea are prepared by steeping plant parts in hot water. Other drinks are made by nature: orange, lemon, and grape juice; coconut milk; apple cider; and apricot nectar are examples. Some beverages come from processed plants. For example, the cola drinks are made from the kola nut of tropical America.

Reading Time _____

Recalling Facts

1. Scientists have named
   - ❏ a. 100 different kinds of plants.
   - ❏ b. 2,000 different kinds of plants.
   - ❏ c. 500,000 different kinds of plants.

2. The chief food plants in North America are
   - ❏ a. seasonings.
   - ❏ b. cereal grains.
   - ❏ c. legumes.

3. Legumes include
   - ❏ a. wheat and rice.
   - ❏ b. peas and peanuts.
   - ❏ c. thyme and sage.

4. Cola drinks are made from
   - ❏ a. the kola nut.
   - ❏ b. cocoa.
   - ❏ c. coconuts.

5. Coffee and tea are prepared by
   - ❏ a. baking plants.
   - ❏ b. grinding the roots of plants.
   - ❏ c. steeping plant parts in hot water.

Understanding Ideas

6. You can conclude from the article that human beings
   - ❏ a. could not survive without plants.
   - ❏ b. need plants to breathe.
   - ❏ c. are discovering new plants every day.

7. The article wants you to understand that plants
   - ❏ a. indirectly provide people with animal products.
   - ❏ b. are not as important as animals.
   - ❏ c. are by-products of animals.

8. You can conclude that places where plants do not grow
   - ❏ a. are very rainy.
   - ❏ b. lack sunlight, air, or soil.
   - ❏ c. are cold.

9. You can conclude that the diets of people in different cultures depend on
   - ❏ a. the types of plants grown locally.
   - ❏ b. crop rotation.
   - ❏ c. scientists.

10. The article suggests that as new plants are discovered,
    - ❏ a. familiar plants will become less useful.
    - ❏ b. new plants will take the place of old plants.
    - ❏ c. there is tremendous potential for expanding people's knowledge of plants.

The Tomato

Tomatoes are plants native to the Americas. They were unknown in Europe until early European explorers of the Americas returned home with them. In Europe, cooks correctly identified the tomato plants as a member of the nightshade family. Nightshade plants were known to be poisonous, and people were especially suspicious of fruits that were red. Europeans considered tomatoes curiosities, not food.

Many early European settlers in the Americas did grow tomatoes, but usually only as ornamental plants. Even in the mid-1800s, people grew tomatoes in their flower gardens for their pretty red fruits. No one ever dreamed of eating one. But gradually word got out that tomatoes were edible if they were cooked for a long time. Cooks would stew them with half a cup of sugar in a tin cup at the back of the wood stove. Still many people were afraid to eat them. One husband of the 1880s came home to find his wife concocting a tomato dish. "Get rid of that—do you want to kill us all?" he thundered.

But tomatoes caught on, and today people eat tomatoes raw or cooked in stews, soups, or sauces. They eat tomatoes alone or in combination with other foods. It's hard to imagine a time—not so very long ago—when tomatoes were not considered a delicious, versatile food.

1. **Recognizing Words in Context**

Find the word *stew* in the passage. One definition below is a *synonym* for that word; it means the same or almost the same thing. One definition is an *antonym;* it has the opposite or nearly opposite meaning. The other has a completely different meaning. Label the definitions S for *synonym,* A for *antonym,* and D for *different.*

_____ a. freeze

_____ b. boil

_____ c. worry

2. **Distinguishing Fact from Opinion**

Two of the statements below present *facts,* which can be proved correct. The other statement is an *opinion,* which expresses someone's thoughts or beliefs. Label the statements F for *fact* and O for *opinion.*

_____ a. Tomato plants are native to the Americas.

_____ b. Tomatoes were poisonous.

_____ c. Tomatoes are a member of the nightshade family.

3. Keeping Events in Order

Label the statements below 1, 2, and 3 to show the order in which the events happened.

_____ a. People grew tomatoes in their gardens as ornamental plants.

_____ b. Tomatoes caught on as a popular food.

_____ c. Early explorers returned to Europe with tomatoes.

4. Making Correct Inferences

Two of the statements below are correct *inferences*, or reasonable guesses. They are based on information in the passage. The other statement is an incorrect, or faulty, inference. Label the statements C for *correct* inference and F for *faulty* inference.

_____ a. People tend to be suspicious of new foods.

_____ b. Tomatoes were potentially harmful to people in the 1800s.

_____ c. Tomatoes have become a very popular food.

5. Understanding Main Ideas

One of the statements below expresses the main idea of the passage. One statement is too general, or too broad. The other explains only part of the passage; it is too narrow. Label the statements M for *main idea*, B for *too broad*, and N for *too narrow*.

_____ a. People develop incorrect ideas about food plants.

_____ b. Early explorers took tomatoes to Europe, but people feared that they were poisonous.

_____ c. The tomato, now in wide use, was long considered something that should not be eaten.

Correct Answers, Part A _____

Correct Answers, Part B _____

Total Correct Answers _____

The world's progress is due largely to inventions. Whenever a new method, machine, or gadget is invented, it helps people live a little easier, better, or longer. Bit by bit, inventors add to wealth, knowledge, and comfort.

Inventors work with known things and known principles. They combine these in a different way to make a new product or process. A discovery differs from an invention. A discovery is something found in nature that was previously unknown to people. A new chemical substance is an example of a discovery. A new type of engine is an example of an invention.

Today inventions are being made in the mechanical, chemical, electronic, and nuclear fields as well as others. New machines and new medicines are developed. New ways of communicating and new uses of energy sources appear often. New inventions lead to new jobs, businesses, and industries. They bring wealth to a nation and help prepare the way for still more inventions.

Invention began with people themselves. Long centuries before the invention of writing, people had invented many important new tools. Among these were fire-making devices, the wheel and axle, the pulley, the saw, the screw, the wedge, and the inclined plane. From these simple machines, a great series of inventions have followed. The wheel, for instance, is the basis for all wheeled things, from roller skates to racing cars. It is used also as a water wheel, a potter's wheel, a steering or controlling device, and part of engines—the flywheel, for example.

In days past, many people lived in villages and worked on farms. They baked clay into pottery and wove rushes into baskets. They spun hair, wool, and flax into thread and wove the thread into cloth. They made axes from stone. After a long time, they learned to smelt metals for tools. In time, they invented weights and measures and ways of telling time and date.

Early people dug wells and irrigation canals. They had drains, sewers, and a water supply to their homes. Gradually, they learned to glaze pottery, work gold and other metals, and make glass for beads. They had lamps for lighting and water clocks for telling time.

Until almost modern times, invention went forward in a hit-or-miss way. There was little science behind it. People progressed only when the need was great and the solution near at hand. Inventions were practical and close to home.

Reading Time _____

Recalling Facts

1. Inventors make new products or processes by
   - ❏ a. working with known things and known principles.
   - ❏ b. making up new principles.
   - ❏ c. finding new things in nature.

2. A discovery is
   - ❏ a. a kind of invention.
   - ❏ b. something found in nature that was formerly unknown.
   - ❏ c. an unnatural process.

3. Roller skates are based on the invention of the
   - ❏ a. wheel.
   - ❏ b. pulley.
   - ❏ c. inclined plane.

4. Among people's earliest inventions were
   - ❏ a. writing implements.
   - ❏ b. clocks.
   - ❏ c. tools.

5. Flax can be
   - ❏ a. smelted for tools.
   - ❏ b. spun into thread.
   - ❏ c. made from stone.

Understanding Ideas

6. Inventions are the result of
   - ❏ a. people's ingenuity.
   - ❏ b. events in nature.
   - ❏ c. natural discoveries.

7. The article suggests that inventions
   - ❏ a. make living conditions worse.
   - ❏ b. improve living conditions.
   - ❏ c. have no effect on living conditions.

8. Compared to earlier inventions, today's inventions are
   - ❏ a. less logical.
   - ❏ b. based on need.
   - ❏ c. more scientific in origin.

9. An example of an invention is
   - ❏ a. a novel made into a film.
   - ❏ b. the computer.
   - ❏ c. a cure for cancer.

10. The next important invention
    - ❏ a. will most likely be in the field of industry.
    - ❏ b. will most likely be atomic in nature.
    - ❏ c. could be in any field.

Fire chiefs from around the country gathered in New Orleans, Louisiana, in October 1914 for an unusual demonstration. The chiefs stood in front of a smoke-filled tent. A local newspaper described the foul-smelling smoke as "thick enough to strangle an elephant."

An organizer introduced the person conducting the demonstration as Big Chief Mason. Big Chief Mason put a canvas hood over his head, walked into the smoky tent, and closed the flap. Twenty minutes later, he came out. He removed the hood and said that he felt as good as new.

The demonstration was given by the National Safety Device Company of Cleveland to advertise its new safety hood. Two hoses connected to the hood reached to the ground. Because smoke rises, there is usually a layer of clean air near the ground. The hood let its wearer breathe this clean air and stay safe from the smoke. Impressed by the demonstration, several of the fire chiefs bought the hood for their departments.

Big Chief Mason was really Garrett Morgan—the inventor of the hood. Morgan posed as a Native American because he had learned that some people would not buy a product invented by an African American. The hood was just one of Morgan's many inventions. He also invented a traffic signal with red, yellow, and green lights.

1. **Recognizing Words in Context**

   Find the word *impressed* in the passage. One definition below is a *synonym* for that word; it means the same or almost the same thing. One definition is an *antonym;* it has the opposite or nearly opposite meaning. The other has a completely different meaning. Label the definitions S for *synonym*, A for *antonym,* and D for *different.*

   _____ a. imprinted

   _____ b. strongly affected

   _____ c. unmoved

2. **Distinguishing Fact from Opinion**

   Two of the statements below present *facts,* which can be proved correct. The other statement is an *opinion,* which expresses someone's thoughts or beliefs. Label the statements F for *fact* and O for *opinion.*

   _____ a. It is not right that Garrett Morgan had to hide the fact that he was an African American.

   _____ b. Garrett Morgan was the inventor of the safety hood.

   _____ c. Morgan was introduced to the fire chiefs as Big Chief Mason.

3. Keeping Events in Order

Two of the statements below describe events that happened at the same time. The other statement describes an event that happened before or after those events. Label them S for *same time*, B for *before*, and A for *after*.

_____ a. Big Chief Mason closed the flap of the tent.

_____ b. Big Chief Mason put a hood over his head and entered a smoke-filled tent.

_____ c. Garrett Morgan invented a safety hood.

4. Making Correct Inferences

Two of the statements below are correct *inferences*, or reasonable guesses. They are based on information in the passage. The other statement is an incorrect, or faulty, inference. Label the statements C for *correct* inference and F for *faulty* inference.

_____ a. No fire chiefs would have bought the safety hood if they had known its inventor was an African American.

_____ b. The fire chiefs thought the safety hood would help keep their firefighters safe from smoke.

_____ c. Garrett Morgan wanted to make sure his invention was not rejected because of his race.

5. Understanding Main Ideas

One of the statements below expresses the main idea of the passage. One statement is too general, or too broad. The other explains only part of the passage; it is too narrow. Label the statements M for *main idea*, B for *too broad*, and N for *too narrow*.

_____ a. Big Chief Mason stayed inside the smoke-filled tent for twenty minutes.

_____ b. Garrett Morgan, an African American, invented a safety hood to protect people from smoke.

_____ c. African-American inventors had difficulty marketing their products because of prejudice.

Correct Answers, Part A _____

Correct Answers, Part B _____

Total Correct Answers _____

The "iron horse" that pulls railroad passenger or freight cars is a power plant on wheels, complete in itself. The term *locomotive* is used for this type of power plant only when it can be uncoupled from the rail cars. Some power plants are part of a passenger car. They may be self-propelled rail-diesel cars. Others could be streamlined electric trains. The term *locomotive* is not used to refer to these power plants.

Until the 1950s, the steam engine locomotive ruled supreme. In North America, Europe, and much of the rest of the world, the steam locomotive has since been replaced by the diesel-electric locomotive. In areas of high rail traffic, as along the East Coast of the United States and in Central Europe, many rail lines have been electrified and use electric locomotives. Today, steam engines are used only in countries, such as China, where coal is much cheaper or more readily available than oil.

Many large locomotives actually develop enough power to supply a small city. Most of the time, however, only a small fraction of this power is needed to pull a train. Once it is underway, a train needs only a few pounds of pulling power to keep one ton of its weight in motion. Full power is needed at first to start the train and then to pull it up a steep grade. To start a long train, the locomotive first backs up to loosen the couplings between cars. In this way, one car after the other begins moving forward. A long string of tightly coupled rail cars cannot be moved all at once.

The old steam locomotive is driven by a steam engine. Steam from the boiler is fed to the engine's cylinders to move pistons back and forth. Connecting rods from the pistons then move the driving wheels. The firebox at the rear end of the boiler is fed with coal or oil. In a large loco-motive, the coal or oil is stored in a tender, or a separate, attached rail car. The tender also holds the water that is turned into steam. The exhaust from the steam cylinders is directed up the smokestack to create a heavy draft for the boiler fire. The discharge of the used steam from the cylinders is con-trolled by valves. The stop-and-go release of the steam up the stack makes the noise that is called the locomotive's puffing.

Reading Time _____

Recalling Facts

1. An "iron horse"
   - ❏ a. pulls railroad passenger or freight cars.
   - ❏ b. produces electricity for railroad cars.
   - ❏ c. provides steam for railroad cars.

2. The term *locomotive* refers to a power plant that
   - ❏ a. is a part of a railroad passenger car.
   - ❏ b. can be uncoupled from railroad cars.
   - ❏ c. is a self-propelled passenger car.

3. To keep one ton of a train's weight in motion, a locomotive must supply
   - ❏ a. full power.
   - ❏ b. an equal amount of pulling power.
   - ❏ c. a few pounds of pulling power.

4. A locomotive's puffing sound comes from
   - ❏ a. wheel action on railroad tracks.
   - ❏ b. pistons moving back and forth.
   - ❏ c. the stop-and-go release of steam up the smokestack.

5. Until the 1950s, most locomotives were driven by
   - ❏ a. electricity.
   - ❏ b. steam.
   - ❏ c. diesel fuel.

Understanding Ideas

6. You can conclude from the article that steam engine locomotives are probably
   - ❏ a. easier to run than diesel-electric locomotives.
   - ❏ b. less efficient than diesel-electric locomotives.
   - ❏ c. making a comeback.

7. The article suggests that railroad transportation is
   - ❏ a. losing its popularity.
   - ❏ b. popular around the world.
   - ❏ c. more popular than any other kind of transportation.

8. You can conclude that the danger of fire is
   - ❏ a. less likely with electric locomotives.
   - ❏ b. more likely with electric locomotives.
   - ❏ c. completely eliminated with electric locomotives.

9. It is likely that in China steam engines will
   - ❏ a. continue to be used for some time.
   - ❏ b. be replaced by electric locomotives.
   - ❏ c. become more expensive to run than engines requiring oil.

10. You can conclude that the power produced by locomotives
    - ❏ a. should be greatly reduced to save energy.
    - ❏ b. is greater than is needed most of the time.
    - ❏ c. is inadequate to drive trains efficiently.

Born in 1864, Casey Jones got his license as a railroad engineer when he was just 26. Friendly, good-natured, and easy to work with, Jones was highly regarded. His trademark was his special whistle. Everyone knew when Jones's train was coming through.

After twelve years, Jones got a plum assignment—the Illinois Central's *Cannonball Express,* a passenger train running between New Orleans and Chicago. On the night of April 29, 1900, Jones arrived in Memphis, heading for New Orleans. The engineer due to take over the train was sick, so Jones and his crew continued on. Ninety minutes late leaving Memphis, they steadily made up time. They hoped to make the next stop on schedule.

It was a miserable, foggy night. Other trains were backed up on a siding near Vaughan, Mississippi. Jones had priority. He poured on steam to go through. But on the track sat the last four cars of a freight that had not made it completely onto the siding. Jones called to the fire stoker, "You jump—I'll stay." Jones tried bravely to stop his train as it headed for destruction. The passengers were only slightly shaken up. Casey Jones was killed.

One of the surviving crew members wrote a song about his engineer. "Casey Jones" became one of the railroad's most enduring ballads.

1. **Recognizing Words in Context**

   Find the word *due* in the passage. One definition below is a *synonym* for that word; it means the same or almost the same thing. One definition is an *antonym;* it has the opposite or nearly opposite meaning. The other has a completely different meaning. Label the definitions S for *synonym,* A for *antonym,* and D for *different.*

   _____ a. unexpected

   _____ b. owed

   _____ c. scheduled

2. **Distinguishing Fact from Opinion**

   Two of the statements below present *facts,* which can be proved correct. The other statement is an *opinion,* which expresses someone's thoughts or beliefs. Label the statements F for *fact* and O for *opinion.*

   _____ a. Casey Jones is the bravest railroad engineer who ever lived.

   _____ b. Casey Jones was born in 1864.

   _____ c. The *Cannonball Express* crashed near Vaughan, Mississippi.

3. Keeping Events in Order

Label the statements below 1, 2, and 3 to show the order in which the events happened.

_____ a. Jones and his crew arrived in Memphis.

_____ b. The *Cannonball Express* hit a freight train.

_____ c. Jones told the fire stoker to jump.

4. Making Correct Inferences

Two of the statements below are correct *inferences*, or reasonable guesses. They are based on information in the passage. The other statement is an incorrect, or faulty, inference. Label the statements C for *correct* inference and F for *faulty* inference.

_____ a. The accident happened because of Casey Jones's recklessness.

_____ b. Casey Jones took his job seriously.

_____ c. Casey Jones valued the lives of his passengers and crew more than his own.

5. Understanding Main Ideas

One of the statements below expresses the main idea of the passage. One statement is too general, or too broad. The other explains only part of the passage; it is too narrow. Label the statements M for *main idea*, B for *too broad*, and N for *too narrow*.

_____ a. Casey Jones, the hero of a ballad, was a railroad engineer killed in a crash while saving his crew and passengers.

_____ b. Many ballads tell the stories of real people and real events.

_____ c. The crash of the *Cannonball Express* occurred on a foggy night when a freight train was unable to make it onto a siding.

Correct Answers, Part A _____

Correct Answers, Part B _____

Total Correct Answers _____

The Birthplace of Human Beings

People can only guess where human beings first appeared on the earth. In this case, *guessing* means drawing a conclusion from all the facts that can be found. The conclusion may fit the known facts, but it cannot be proved by the actual evidence. A commonly accepted conclusion is that Asia is the birthplace of humans.

There are facts that support this conclusion. People may have developed from an apelike ancestor common to humans and other primates. The lands where animals have developed over thousands of years have had mild climates, various kinds of landscapes, and enough, but not too much, food.

At a point in time, a few million years before humans appeared, there was a vast plateau in northern Asia. The climate there was neither cold nor tropical. When not searching for food, animals would not have just rested all of the time. They would have been roving around because new sources of food would have to be found. On this plateau, there were forests, plains, and open land. Some of these places had plenty of rain. Others were deserts. Many of the plants were good to eat, and there was plenty of game.

The very earliest humans probably dwelled on the floor of the forests. There they could use the trees as shelters. Those who ventured onto the plains had to be alert to avoid the floods and sandstorms that caught and preserved so many animals. Ability to escape provided for future generations, but left no evidence of the past.

There were primates in Asia before the earliest records of humans. The primates were different from the primates and humans of today, but they could have been the ancestors of either or both.

The first of the human creatures was found in Asia, and the greatest number of possible ancestors was also found there. Asia seems a probable homeland for humanity.

However, there is room for disagreement. No one disputes that humans could have been able to develop in Asia. But researchers point out that the same conditions on other continents could have led to the same development. Africa is one example. Conditions there were much the same in ancient times. Moreover, the most humanlike apes live there today.

People will have to wait for the discovery of more fossil bones and the study of them before they can know positively which continent was the birthplace of humans.

Reading Time _____

Recalling Facts

1. A likely place for humans' first appearance is
   - ❏ a. South America.
   - ❏ b. Asia.
   - ❏ c. Australia.

2. It is possible that humans descended from
   - ❏ a. early plants.
   - ❏ b. fossils.
   - ❏ c. primates.

3. One argument that favors Africa as the birthplace of humans states that
   - ❏ a. the most humanlike apes live there today.
   - ❏ b. more fossil bones are found there.
   - ❏ c. much of Africa is desert.

4. The first humans probably
   - ❏ a. lived on the floor of the forest.
   - ❏ b. were desert dwellers.
   - ❏ c. were tree dwellers.

5. Conclusions about human beings' birthplace are based on
   - ❏ a. imaginative guesses.
   - ❏ b. available facts.
   - ❏ c. the discovery of ancient writings.

Understanding Ideas

6. The earliest humans probably fared best in
   - ❏ a. tropical climates.
   - ❏ b. cold climates.
   - ❏ c. mild climates.

7. You can conclude from the article that scientists
   - ❏ a. have determined the location of humans' birthplace.
   - ❏ b. will continue to investigate humans' birthplace.
   - ❏ c. have determined little about humans' birthplace.

8. You can conclude that the determination of humans' birthplace depends largely on
   - ❏ a. new discoveries.
   - ❏ b. guesswork.
   - ❏ c. reexamining known facts.

9. You can conclude that the environment of present-day Africa
   - ❏ a. is different from that of northern Asia in the past.
   - ❏ b. cannot be compared to that of northern Asia in the past.
   - ❏ c. is similar to that of northern Asia in the past.

10. The article suggests that the final determination of humans' birthplace
    - ❏ a. will probably never be made.
    - ❏ b. is likely to be made someday.
    - ❏ c. should remain a mystery.

Looking for Lucy

In 1974, Donald Johanson and a team of anthropologists discovered parts of a skeleton at Hadar in Ethiopia. They estimated it to be about 3.2 million years old. The skeleton appeared to be from an unknown species. It was neither an ape nor a human but something in between. Johanson named his find Lucy and gave this new species the scientific name *Australopithecus afarensis.*

There was one big problem with the Lucy skeleton. It had a jawbone, but it had no skull. A skull would have provided a great deal of information about Lucy. Scientists argued about whether Johanson had really found a new species. Some researchers charged that he had mixed up bones from two different species.

In 1993, Yoel Rak, a member of the 1974 team, was back in Ethiopia. While walking along a gully, Rak saw bits of bone. Following the gully, he soon located an upper jawbone and parts of a skull. Rak began to shout excitedly to the rest of the team. The researchers planned a thorough excavation of the hillside. When the digging and sorting were over, they had a nearly complete *A. afarensis* skull—just what they had been hoping for. "Lucy," someone remarked, "finally has a head."

1. **Recognizing Words in Context**

   Find the word *charged* in the passage. One definition below is a *synonym* for that word; it means the same or almost the same thing. One definition is an *antonym;* it has the opposite or nearly opposite meaning. The other has a completely different meaning. Label the definitions S for *synonym,* A for *antonym,* and D for *different.*

   _____ a. accused
   _____ b. stampeded
   _____ c. approved

2. **Distinguishing Fact from Opinion**

   Two of the statements below present *facts,* which can be proved correct. The other statement is an *opinion,* which expresses someone's thoughts or beliefs. Label the statements F for *fact* and O for *opinion.*

   _____ a. Johanson had mixed up bones from two different species.
   _____ b. The Lucy skeleton had a jawbone but no skull.
   _____ c. Yoel Rak found an *A. afarensis* skull.

3. Keeping Events in Order

Label the statements below 1, 2, and 3 to show the order in which the events happened.

_____ a. Yoel Rak found pieces of a skull.

_____ b. Donald Johanson found a skeleton he named Lucy.

_____ c. Scientists argued whether Lucy was really from a new species.

4. Making Correct Inferences

Two of the statements below are correct *inferences,* or reasonable guesses. They are based on information in the passage. The other statement is an incorrect, or faulty, inference. Label the statements C for *correct* inference and F for *faulty* inference.

_____ a. The Lucy skeleton shows that humans originated in Ethiopia.

_____ b. The skeleton of Lucy was an important scientific discovery.

_____ c. Anthropologists work to expand our knowledge of human origins.

5. Understanding Main Ideas

One of the statements below expresses the main idea of the passage. One statement is too general, or too broad. The other explains only part of the passage; it is too narrow. Label the statements M for *main idea*, B for *too broad*, and N for *too narrow*.

_____ a. Twenty years after finding a partial skeleton of a new prehuman species, a team of anthropologists found a skull that proved their claim.

_____ b. Anthropologists study human beings and their origins.

_____ c. Scientists argued about whether Johanson had really found a new species or had mixed up the bones of two different species.

Correct Answers, Part A _____

Correct Answers, Part B _____

Total Correct Answers _____

Thomas Jefferson was the third president of the United States. He was also the author of the Declaration of Independence and the Virginia Statute for Religious Freedom. In an age of greatness, Jefferson was noted for his curious mind. He was a farmer, scientist, architect, and inventor as well as a government leader. He helped the United States get started, and his plans for the future helped it grow. Many of the good things Americans enjoy today have come from Jefferson's devotion to human rights.

Jefferson was a tall, straight-bodied, loose-jointed person. He stood and walked straight and his shoulders were always square. He had hazel eyes and a long, high nose. No one ever thought of him as handsome. His hair was reddish, becoming sandy as he grew older. Unlike other gentlemen of his day, he never wore a wig.

In the fashion of his time, Jefferson dressed in a long, dark coat; a ruffled cravat (in place of the modern necktie); a red waistcoat, short knee breeches; and shoes with big, bright buckles. Except in his days of courtship and married life, he paid little attention to clothes. When he was president of the United States, Jefferson made a habit of plainness, both in his personal appearance and in matters of ceremony.

Jefferson was a courteous person, bowing to everyone he met. He was reserved, and no one ever called him by his first name. He was a very poor public speaker in a day of great orators. He talked in a thin, fine voice.

He loved music, played the violin well, liked to sing, and usually hummed or sang as he walked or rode. A good horseback rider, he often rode for pleasure when people generally rode only as a means of travel.

About 37 years after Jefferson's death, Abraham Lincoln described the American government as "of the people, by the people, for the people." He was defining the kind of government that Jefferson, more than any other official, had made possible. Even Jefferson's closest coworkers thought of human rights as including the protection of life and liberty and, above all, of private property. Their use of the words "all men are created equal" left out racial minorities. There is much evidence that Jefferson did not exclude them.

"Give the people light," said Jefferson, "and they will find their own way." He meant all the people.

Reading Time _____

Recalling Facts

1. Thomas Jefferson was the United States'
   - ❏ a. first president.
   - ❏ b. second president.
   - ❏ c. third president.

2. Thomas Jefferson was not an author of the
   - ❏ a. Declaration of Independence.
   - ❏ b. Constitution of the United States.
   - ❏ c. Virginia Statute for Religious Freedom.

3. Jefferson was known
   - ❏ a. as a fine orator.
   - ❏ b. for his devotion to human rights.
   - ❏ c. as an open, friendly person.

4. Jefferson could play
   - ❏ a. a variety of musical instruments.
   - ❏ b. the guitar.
   - ❏ c. the violin well.

5. Most gentlemen of Jefferson's time
   - ❏ a. cared little about their appearance.
   - ❏ b. did not wear wigs.
   - ❏ c. wore red vests and bright shoe buckles.

Understanding Ideas

6. The characteristic that most qualified Thomas Jefferson for the presidency was probably his
   - ❏ a. curious mind.
   - ❏ b. horse riding ability.
   - ❏ c. plainness.

7. You can conclude from the article that the Declaration of Independence guaranteed Americans
   - ❏ a. human rights.
   - ❏ b. wealth.
   - ❏ c. a strong government.

8. You can conclude that Thomas Jefferson was a talented
   - ❏ a. singer.
   - ❏ b. writer.
   - ❏ c. public speaker.

9. If Thomas Jefferson were alive today, he would most likely support
   - ❏ a. educational scholarships.
   - ❏ b. the fashion industry.
   - ❏ c. a dictator.

10. You can conclude that Jefferson's ideas about government
    - ❏ a. agreed with those of his coworkers.
    - ❏ b. would be unacceptable today.
    - ❏ c. were ahead of his time.

If anyone ever needed a copying machine, it was Thomas Jefferson. Jefferson constantly wrote in his notebooks. He wrote many letters to friends about his experiences. To be sure he would not forget what he had written, he made copies of his letters for his files.

The British inventor James Watt had invented a copier, although it was awkward to use. Writing had to be done in special, slow-drying ink. Tissue paper was then pressed onto the wet ink to make the copy. Because the copy was a mirror image of the original, it had to be read from the back.

Jefferson got one of Watt's machines and immediately began tinkering with it. He eventually made a copier small enough to fit into his laptop desk. He used this copier for twenty years.

In the early 1800s, Jefferson found a new invention called a polygraph. It linked five pens together with rods. Each pen touched a sheet of paper. Jefferson could write with one pen, and the other four pens made the same movements. All the copies looked the same, and they could be made on high-quality paper. Each time Jefferson wrote, he produced an original and four good copies.

Today, electronic copiers crank out hundreds of copies in seconds. Jefferson would be delighted.

1. **Recognizing Words in Context**

   Find the word *awkward* in the passage. One definition below is a *synonym* for that word; it means the same or almost the same thing. One definition is an *antonym;* it has the opposite or nearly opposite meaning. The other has a completely different meaning. Label the definitions S for *synonym,* A for *antonym,* and D for *different.*

   _____ a. uncomfortable

   _____ b. inconvenient

   _____ c. handy

2. **Distinguishing Fact from Opinion**

   Two of the statements below present *facts,* which can be proved correct. The other statement is an *opinion,* which expresses someone's thoughts or beliefs. Label the statements F for *fact* and O for *opinion.*

   _____ a. James Watt invented a copier.

   _____ b. Jefferson would be thrilled with today's copiers.

   _____ c. Jefferson made use of a new invention called a polygraph.

3. Keeping Events in Order

Two of the statements below describe events that happened at the same time. The other statement describes an event that happened before or after those events. Label them S for *same time,* B for *before,* and A for *after.*

_____ a. Jefferson used an improved version of Watt's invention to make copies.

_____ b. Jefferson wrote a letter with one pen of the polygraph.

_____ c. The polygraph's other four pens made an exact copy of the letter.

4. Making Correct Inferences

Two of the statements below are correct *inferences,* or reasonable guesses. They are based on information in the passage. The other statement is an incorrect, or faulty, inference. Label the statements C for *correct* inference and F for *faulty* inference.

_____ a. Jefferson was always looking for better ways to make copies.

_____ b. Jefferson was satisfied with Watt's invention.

_____ c. Jefferson liked new inventions.

5. Understanding Main Ideas

One of the statements below expresses the main idea of the passage. One statement is too general, or too broad. The other explains only part of the passage; it is too narrow. Label the statements M for *main idea,* B for *too broad,* and N for *too narrow.*

_____ a. A writer who made many copies, Thomas Jefferson first used James Watt's copier, which he improved on, and later a polygraph.

_____ b. Thomas Jefferson tinkered with Watt's copier to make it small enough to fit into his laptop desk.

_____ c. Thomas Jefferson was noted for his wide-ranging curiosity on many subjects.

Correct Answers, Part A _____

Correct Answers, Part B _____

Total Correct Answers _____

Clothing, a Basic Need

Like food and shelter, clothing is a basic human need. One reason people began wearing clothing was for protection. Rough garments protected them from animal bites, scratches, and burns. Clothing also kept the people warm and dry.

People still wear protective clothing for some types of work and play. The construction worker's hard hat, the chemist's rubber gloves, and the football player's shoulder pads and helmet help protect against injury. The average person may not need special clothing to keep him or her from being hurt. But most people do need warm coats, waterproof overshoes, and sun hats for protection against the weather.

Climate affects the amount and types of clothing that people wear. Those who live in hot, humid African countries may wear very little clothing. If air can flow freely to their skin, perspiration moisture dries more quickly. This helps dispose of body heat.

Many Arabs live in a climate that is hot but dry. Unlike the people of Africa, they wear traditional clothing that covers them from head to toe. Their loose white wool robes reflect the sun's rays and shield them from the hot winds. Such garments also provide insulation against the nighttime cold.

Inuits in Canada and Alaska traditionally wear two layers of clothing, usually sealskin or caribou furs. The inner layer consists of undergarments and socks. The hairy side of undergarments is worn against the skin. Outer garments—trousers, hooded parka, mittens, and boots—are worn with the hairy side out.

People who live in mild climates vary their clothing with the seasons. The clothes they wear in summer are usually loosely woven and light in weight. In winter, they may wear extra layers of clothing to hold in the warmth of their bodies. They may also wear a coat of closely woven cloth, leather, or fur to insulate them against the cold.

In recent years, garments have been made to protect people from temperatures more extreme than any encountered on Earth. The space suits worn by the astronauts enable them to function comfortably at widely ranging temperatures, in sunlight or in shade.

Clothing is also worn for reasons other than shelter from heat and cold. One of the most important reasons is appearance. People choose clothes that they like and that they think other people will like. They try to select clothes in styles and colors that look good to them and to others.

Reading Time _____

Recalling Facts

1. People began wearing clothing for
   - ❏ a. decoration.
   - ❏ b. protection.
   - ❏ c. amusement.

2. The amount and types of clothing people wear are affected by
   - ❏ a. air pollution.
   - ❏ b. work habits.
   - ❏ c. climate.

3. The loose, white wool robes worn by Arabs help
   - ❏ a. reflect the sun's rays.
   - ❏ b. allow hot winds to flow through.
   - ❏ c. provide warmth during cool summers.

4. Inuit clothing usually consists of
   - ❏ a. wool.
   - ❏ b. animal skins or furs.
   - ❏ c. cotton.

5. To help keep warm during cold winter months, people wear
   - ❏ a. loosely knit clothing.
   - ❏ b. lightweight clothing.
   - ❏ c. layers of clothing.

Understanding Ideas

6. If moisture from perspiration dries quickly, body temperature is likely to
   - ❏ a. drop.
   - ❏ b. rise.
   - ❏ c. stay the same.

7. In hot, humid climates, people are likely to wear
   - ❏ a. more clothing.
   - ❏ b. less clothing.
   - ❏ c. tight clothing.

8. Based on what you know about white clothing, you would expect darker clothing to
   - ❏ a. retain moisture.
   - ❏ b. reflect heat.
   - ❏ c. absorb heat.

9. You can conclude from the article that how people appear to others is
   - ❏ a. not important to most people.
   - ❏ b. a concern to most people.
   - ❏ c. has little to do with clothing.

10. Clothing made for astronauts must be
   - ❏ a. adaptable.
   - ❏ b. cool.
   - ❏ c. heavy.

25 | B | Birth of the Blues—Blue Jeans, That Is

A young German immigrant named Levi Strauss arrived in San Francisco in the 1850s. He brought with him a large supply of canvas that he planned to sell to miners for tents and wagon covers. He soon found, however, that what the miners really needed were tough work pants. Nothing that was available at the time could hold up to hard use in the mines. Seeing an opportunity to meet a need, Strauss had a tailor sew the canvas into work pants. The pants were an instant success.

Strauss ordered more cloth from his brothers, who owned a dry-goods business in New York. Instead of canvas, they sent him a tough French cotton called *serge de Nimes*. San Franciscans soon shortened the name to denim. Another denimlike fabric, named *Gênes* by the French, gave Strauss's new product a name that has stuck—jeans.

Miners complained that the pockets of the pants often ripped out when stuffed with rocks and tools. Strauss's tailor suggested using copper rivets to strengthen the pockets. The change was a big hit with miners and other workers.

At first, jeans were a drab, brown color. This was the natural color of the fabric. Strauss thought his pants would sell better if the color were brighter. He began dying the cloth a deep blue—and blue jeans were born.

1. **Recognizing Words in Context**

   Find the word *hit* in the passage. One definition below is a *synonym* for that word; it means the same or almost the same thing. One definition is an *antonym;* it has the opposite or nearly opposite meaning. The other has a completely different meaning. Label the definitions below S for *synonym*, A for *antonym,* and D for *different*.

   _____ a. success

   _____ b. strike

   _____ c. failure

2. **Distinguishing Fact from Opinion**

   Two of the statements below present *facts,* which can be proved correct. The other statement is an *opinion,* which expresses someone's thoughts or beliefs. Label the statements F for *fact* and O for *opinion*.

   _____ a. The word *jeans* comes from the French word *Gênes*.

   _____ b. Blue jeans were an important invention.

   _____ c. Strauss's first work pants were made of canvas.

3. Keeping Events in Order

Label the statements below 1, 2, and 3 to show the order in which the events happened.

_____ a. San Franciscans called the fabric denim.

_____ b. Strauss had canvas made into work pants.

_____ c. Strauss dyed the fabric a deep blue.

4. Making Correct Inferences

Two of the statements below are correct *inferences*, or reasonable guesses. They are based on information in the passage. The other statement is an incorrect, or faulty, inference. Label the statements C for *correct* inference and F for *faulty* inference.

_____ a. Strauss was successful because he saw a need and met it.

_____ b. The miners were pleased with Strauss's work pants.

_____ c. The best cloth for jeans comes from France.

5. Understanding Main Ideas

One of the statements below expresses the main idea of the passage. One statement is too general, or too broad. The other explains only part of the passage; it is too narrow. Label the statements M for *main idea*, B for *too broad*, and N for *too narrow*.

_____ a. Clothing is a basic human need.

_____ b. Strauss's brothers sent him French cotton called serge de Nimes.

_____ c. A German immigrant named Levi Strauss invented blue jeans in California.

Correct Answers, Part A _____

Correct Answers, Part B _____

Total Correct Answers _____

Answer Key

Reading Rate Graph

Comprehension Score Graph

Comprehension Skills Profile Graph

Answer Key

1A	1. a	2. a	3. b	4. c	5. b	6. b	7. c	8. b	9. c	10. b
1B	1. D, A, S		2. O, F, F		3. 3, 2, 1		4. C, C, F		5. N, M, B	
2A	1. c	2. c	3. c	4. a	5. b	6. c	7. a	8. c	9. a	10. c
2B	1. D, S, A		2. F, F, O		3. 1, 3, 2		4. F, C, C		5. M, B, N	
3A	1. b	2. b	3. c	4. b	5. c	6. a	7. b	8. c	9. a	10. a
3B	1. S, A, D		2. F, O, F		3. 2, 1, 3		4. C, F, C		5. B, M, N	
4A	1. c	2. c	3. a	4. c	5. c	6. a	7. b	8. b	9. b	10. a
4B	1. D, S, A		2. F, F, O		3. S, S, B		4. F, C, C		5. B, M, N	
5A	1. c	2. a	3. b	4. c	5. a	6. b	7. c	8. b	9. b	10. b
5B	1. S, A, D		2. F, O, F		3. 1, 2, 3		4. F, C, C		5. M, N, B	
6A	1. a	2. c	3. c	4. a	5. c	6. a	7. b	8. a	9. b	10. c
6B	1. A, D, S		2. F, F, O		3. 2, 3, 1		4. F, C, C		5. B, N, M	
7A	1. c	2. a	3. b	4. b	5. a	6. c	7. a	8. c	9. a	10. a
7B	1. S, A, D		2. F, F, O		3. S, B, S		4. C, C, F		5. N, B, M	
8A	1. b	2. a	3. b	4. a	5. a	6. b	7. c	8. b	9. c	10. c
8B	1. D, A, S		2. F, F, O		3. S, A, S		4. C, F, C		5. B, N, M	
9A	1. b	2. b	3. c	4. c	5. b	6. b	7. a	8. c	9. a	10. a
9B	1. A, S, D		2. O, F, F		3. B, S, S		4. C, F, C		5. N, B, M	
10A	1. b	2. c	3. c	4. b	5. b	6. c	7. b	8. a	9. c	10. a
10B	1. A, S, D		2. F, F, O		3. 3, 2, 1		4. C, C, F		5. M, N, B	
11A	1. b	2. b	3. c	4. a	5. b	6. c	7. c	8. b	9. c	10. b
11B	1. S, A, D		2. F, O, F		3. S, B, S		4. C, F, C		5. B, N, M	
12A	1. b	2. c	3. a	4. b	5. a	6. a	7. b	8. c	9. b	10. c
12B	1. D, S, A		2. F, F, O		3. 2, 1, 3		4. C, F, C		5. N, M, B	
13A	1. b	2. c	3. a	4. b	5. c	6. b	7. b	8. b	9. a	10. c
13B	1. D, S, A		2. F, F, O		3. 1, 2, 3		4. F, C, C		5. B, M, N	

14A	1. a	2. b	3. c	4. b	5. b	6. b	7. c	8. b	9. c	10. a
14B	1. A, D, S		2. O, F, F		3. S, A, S		4. C, C, F		5. M, N, B	
15A	1. a	2. a	3. c	4. b	5. b	6. c	7. c	8. b	9. b	10. a
15B	1. A, S, D		2. F, F, O		3. 2, 3, 1		4. C, C, F		5. B, N, M	
16A	1. a	2. c	3. c	4. a	5. c	6. b	7. b	8. c	9. a	10. b
16B	1. A, D, S		2. F, O, F		3. 3, 1, 2		4. F, C, C		5. M, B, N	
17A	1. b	2. b	3. c	4. a	5. c	6. b	7. c	8. a	9. c	10. b
17B	1. A, D, S		2. F, O, F		3. 1, 3, 2		4. F, C, C		5. M, B, N	
18A	1. a	2. c	3. a	4. b	5. a	6. b	7. a	8. a	9. b	10. a
18B	1. A, S, D		2. F, F, O		3. 2, 1, 3		4. C, F, C		5. N, B, M	
19A	1. b	2. a	3. b	4. b	5. c	6. b	7. b	8. c	9. a	10. a
19B	1. S, A, D		2. O, F, F		3. S, A, S		4. C, C, F		5. N, B, M	
20A	1. c	2. b	3. b	4. a	5. c	6. a	7. a	8. b	9. a	10. c
20B	1. A, S, D		2. F, O, F		3. 2, 3, 1		4. C, F, C		5. B, N, M	
21A	1. a	2. b	3. a	4. c	5. b	6. a	7. b	8. c	9. b	10. c
21B	1. D, S, A		2. O, F, F		3. S, S, B		4. F, C, C		5. N, M, B	
22A	1. a	2. b	3. c	4. c	5. b	6. b	7. b	8. a	9. a	10. b
22B	1. A, D, S		2. O, F, F		3. 1, 3, 2		4. F, C, C		5. M, B, N	
23A	1. b	2. c	3. a	4. a	5. b	6. c	7. b	8. a	9. c	10. c
23B	1. S, D, A		2. O, F, F		3. 3, 1, 2		4. F, C, C		5. M, B, N	
24A	1. c	2. b	3. b	4. c	5. c	6. a	7. a	8. b	9. a	10. c
24B	1. D, S, A		2. F, O, F		3. B, S, S		4. C, F, C		5. M, N, B	
25A	1. b	2. c	3. a	4. b	5. c	6. a	7. b	8. c	9. b	10. a
25B	1. S, D, A		2. F, O, F		3. 2, 1, 3		4. C, C, F		5. B, N, M	

READING RATE

Put an X on the line above each lesson number to show your reading time and words-per-minute rate for that unit.

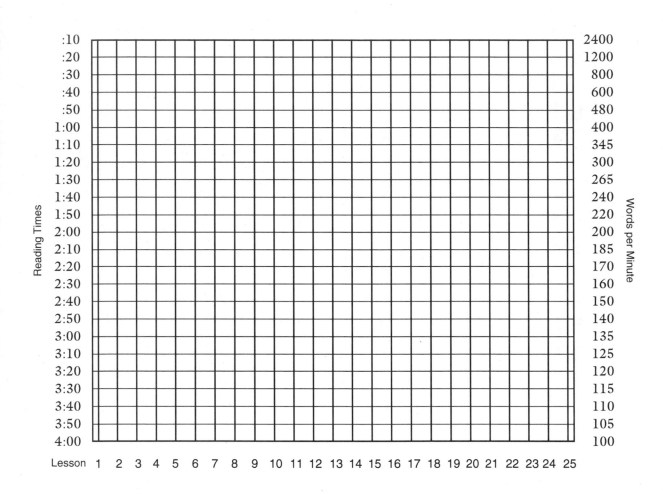

COMPREHENSION SCORE

Put an X on the line above each lesson number to indicate your total correct answers and comprehension score for that unit.

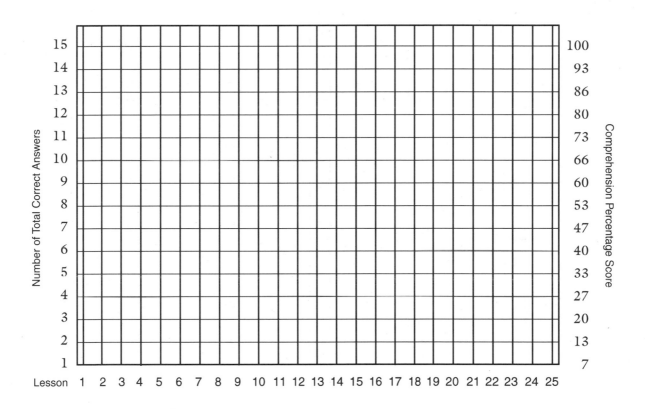

Number of Total Correct Answers

15		100
14		93
13		86
12		80
11		73
10		66
9		60
8		53
7		47
6		40
5		33
4		27
3		20
2		13
1		7

Lesson 1 2 3 4 5 6 7 8 9 10 11 12 13 14 15 16 17 18 19 20 21 22 23 24 25

Comprehension Percentage Score

COMPREHENSION SKILLS PROFILE

Put an X in the box above each question type to indicate an incorrect reponse to any part of that question.

	Recognizing Words in Context	Distinguishing Fact from Opinion	Keeping Events in Order	Making Correct Inferences	Understanding Main Ideas
Lesson 1					
2					
3					
4					
5					
6					
7					
8					
9					
10					
11					
12					
13					
14					
15					
16					
17					
18					
19					
20					
21					
22					
23					
24					
25					